MORE THAN CLAY

living life unashamed

GREG MCKINNEY

FOREWORD BY: NICK T. OGLE, PH.D., LPC

WESTBOW
PRESS®
A DIVISION OF THOMAS NELSON
& ZONDERVAN

This book is a work of non-fiction. Unless otherwise noted, the author and the publisher make no explicit guarantees as to the accuracy of the information contained in this book and in some cases, names of people and places have been altered to protect their privacy.

Scripture quotations taken from the New American Standard Bible˚, Copyright © 1960, 1962, 1963, 1968, 1971, 1972, 1973, 1975, 1977, 1995 by The Lockman Foundation. Used by permission. (www.Lockman.org)

Scripture quotations are from The Holy Bible, English Standard Version® (ESV®), copyright © 2001 by Crossway, a publishing ministry of Good News Publishers. Used by permission. All rights reserved.

Scripture taken from the Holy Bible, NEW INTERNATIONAL VERSION®. Copyright © 1973, 1978, 1984 by Biblica, Inc. All rights reserved worldwide. Used by permission. NEW INTERNATIONAL VERSION® and NIV® are registered trademarks of Biblica, Inc. Use of either trademark for the offering of goods or services requires the prior written consent of Biblica US, Inc.

New Revised Standard Version Bible, copyright © 1989, Division of Christian Education of the National Council of the Churches of Christ in the United States of America. Used by permission. All rights reserved.

WestBow Press books may be ordered through booksellers or by contacting:

WestBow Press
A Division of Thomas Nelson & Zondervan
1663 Liberty Drive
Bloomington, IN 47403
www.westbowpress.com
1 (866) 928-1240

Because of the dynamic nature of the Internet, any web addresses or links contained in this book may have changed since publication and may no longer be valid. The views expressed in this work are solely those of the author and do not necessarily reflect the views of the publisher, and the publisher hereby disclaims any responsibility for them.

Any people depicted in stock imagery provided by Thinkstock are models, and such images are being used for illustrative purposes only. Certain stock imagery © Thinkstock.

ISBN: 978-1-5127-1791-4 (sc)
ISBN: 978-1-5127-1792-1 (hc)
ISBN: 978-1-5127-1790-7 (e)

Library of Congress Control Number: 2015917967

Printed by Bookmasters, Ashland Ohio.

WestBow Press rev. date: 12/09/2015

CONTENTS

To my wonderful wife, who countlessly and gracefully halted her daily tasks in order to hear me ramble through my ideas and stories.

My own battle through shame cannot be adequately described without giving mention to the power and grace that Christ Jesus has continually displayed through her. She is my constant.

FOREWORD

Over the years I have come to learn that one of the most powerful feelings in my life, outside of the feeling of love, is that of shame. It is a confusing feeling because it serves dichotomous roles.

On one hand, it torments me. Shame lies to me, relentlessly telling me I am unworthy or a failure. It works diligently to define my character in ways that destroy my passion, authenticity, and overall ability to be who God created me to be. When shame gets ahold of my heart, I am paralyzed and unable to be used by my Savior.

On the other hand, shame serves as one of the most powerful motivators in my life. When I am able to recognize and speak against the lies of shame, I am able to rise above and allow the Spirit of the Lord to redefine me. Although the feeling of shame loses it power, the core feelings such as unworthiness and failure remain in a redefined manner. In other words, failure and unworthiness no longer *define* me but rather *remind* me of why I am dependent upon the Cross.

More Than Clay is one of the best tools I have discovered to help recognize, battle, and redefine shame in one's life. This book is full of examples, illustrations, and Biblical connections. Page after page, I am challenged to redefine my shame. And in the process I am encouraged to discover a renewed passion for whom the Lord created me to be.

A book like this one could not be written by just anyone. It had to be written by an individual who has walked through dark seasons of shame. This book demanded an author who has learned to hear the voice of the Lord, despite the calling of shame to feel like an unworthy failure. To that end, it makes complete sense to me why God called Greg to write this book. He is a man after God's own heart. He truly has a Davidic spirit! This book will inspire you because it is written from a place of understanding. He captures true feelings of shame because he has learned to recognize them and battle them in his own life.

I am a stronger man—or better yet—a wiser man for having read this book. I am working diligently to apply its principles to recognize, battle, and redefine shame in my life. May this book enrich your life in the same way it has enriched mine.

Blessings,

Nick T. Ogle, Ph.D., LPC

PREFACE

WHAT YOU NEED TO KNOW

But we have this treasure in jars of clay
to show that this all-surpassing power
is from God and not from us.
-2 Corinthians 4:7

We are jars of clay.

Yes. We are made from the dirt and dull in color: jars of clay.

On the outside, we appear pretty simple and ordinary. But inside, deep in the core of who we are, shines something else. You see, scripture tells us that "in Christ" *our clay-ness is no longer the extent of who we are.* It says that inside of us is something that makes us *more* than just a simple jar; something that is truly *extraordinary.*

And that something is the glory of God; the real life experience and evidence of just how great our God is.

But if you are like me, then you, too, are hit with an obstacle.

No matter how often we are told of our new life in Christ, there seems to be a part of us that continually doubts and questions it. No matter how many years are tacked onto my spiritual life, there seems to be something—or someone—that always wants my focus to be elsewhere.

In fact, every day we are met by a voice that leads us to become so caught up in only seeing our outer view of clay that we hardly take notice of the true treasure that is inside.

And if I am completely honest, on the outside, all I tend to see are the cracks, scratches, and dents in my clay—marks made by the choices that I once made. Every one of them provides reminders of my shortcomings. Yet with this perception, I tend to be frozen and fed the lie that all I am is clay or dirt. And this is exactly where the world and my enemy want me to be.

In fact, in this perception, we *all* tend to be frozen and fed these shame-filled lies. But this should not be so.

We are *more than clay.*

And aside from being a pretty neat title, this phrase is also quite pivotal when discussing who we are—who we truly and fundamentally are—as believers and followers of Christ. Because all too often, we get caught up with the belief that we are anything but *more.*

And this is the deceitful work of Satan and the world.

Therefore, this book is aimed at helping you live out the unashamed life that Christ Jesus has given you. In doing this, we will hopefully silence every one of the lies believed from our accuser; the enemy of love, peace, and holiness.

With that said, I have split this book into three sections that, through the lenses of scripture, will allow us to journey out of shame. The first section will uncover what shame truly is, while also shedding light on our "shamer." Then, using scripture, we will dive into the truth of who we are in Christ Jesus. And finally, the last section will provide practical steps on how we can daily live the unashamed life.

Although the first half may feel like a refresher course to many of you, I encourage you to continue on. For the foundational truths in these pages are what enable us to *be* and *act* unashamedly. So for those of you "doers" out there who want to skip right ahead to the action (myself included), please take your time to read through the truth.

And do know that you are not alone in your struggles with shame.

In fact, I have intentionally designed this book to be usable in the context of small groups. So if you can, try to go through it with others. At the end of every chapter, I have provided you with questions to help you reflect and engage with the text in new ways.

But before you begin, I would like to share with you the full passage from 2 Corinthians. Satan wants us to deeply believe that we are disgusting, worthless, vile, and sinful at the core. And because we are stuck here in our flesh, these are very easy lies to believe. But as I said before, we are more than what is outwardly seen.

As you read each chapter and uncover the depth of your own shame, remember to fall back onto the truths in these verses. And hopefully, as you continue on, they will take on a deeper meaning for you.

> For God, who said, "Let light shine out of darkness," made His light shine in our hearts to give us the light of the knowledge of the glory of God in the face of Christ. But we have this treasure in jars of clay to show that this all-surpassing power is from God and not from us. We are hard pressed on every side, but not crushed, perplexed, but not in despair; persecuted, but not abandoned; struck down, but not destroyed. We always carry in our body the death of Jesus, so that the life of Jesus may also be revealed in our body…life is at work in you.
>
> -2 Corinthians 4: 6-10; 12

PART 1

AN AGE OLD DILEMMA

CHAPTER 1

DO YOU FEEL IT?

"Shame is a soul-eating emotion...."
- C.G. Jung

"The feeling of shame is about our very
selves—not about some bad thing we did
or said but about what we are."
- Lewis Smedes

He sat and stared into the bleak night as rain continued to fall on his home. Its consistency was the one thing that seemed to keep his mind at ease after a day like today.

Today was a market day.

To his dread, he had not been able to go another second without consuming some kind of food. After he was cast out from society, the coins collecting dust on the table naturally lost all value. Yes, he needed food to survive, but the means to getting that food was something he utterly despised.

Like always, the pursuit of food meant that he had to trudge through those dusty streets screaming a word that he, deep down, knew defined him. It might as well be his name, seeing as he hadn't spoken his true one in so long.

"Unclean," he whispered into the blackness.

Chills ran down his back as the voice in his head mockingly reminded him of who he had become. Instantly, those taunting and scornful faces from today ran through his mind. Like a disturbing track, the images played over and over. In fact, the very sound of his "name" made the people of Galilee flee to the other side of the street. Although he lived so close to the border of the city, he could not imagine feeling more secluded.

There were once others like him—a man, two women, and a young boy. Their company did seem to subdue the loneliness, but nothing could silence the depth of pain they all felt inside. Due to the severity of their condition, they each, one by one, returned to the dust. His constant memories of them made him wonder and yearn for the day that he, too, would become forever numb. It seemed so natural to him that dirt would return to dirt.

But he deserved this life. Although he was always confused by what the others did to receive this penalty, he knew intensely the disgust of his own ways.

He *deserved* this life.

And hidden deep within his heart was every wrong deed that led him to become the filth that he is. Although he now regarded himself as nothing, it was not a belief that he had always held.

He grew up in Hebrew tradition, where leprosy is taught to be a direct infliction from God; a punishment for horrid crimes. In the beginning, he constantly struggled with why others could commit the same wrongs, yet neglect to receive this shameful disease. What made him so different?

As time passed, however, he came to realize the ignorance of his ways. The "truth" he had come to believe was that others were not rotting because their evil existed on such a lower level than his own. They may have sin, but he *was* sin. In fact, every scornful eye and degrading word only made this fact more concrete. He was a leper—a no good, rotten leper.

Even now, as he sat looking out into the rain, he was what he always had been, and what he would forever be: unlovable, unworthy, and unclean.

And nothing would change that.

SHAME TRAVELS THROUGH ALL ERAS

Every day, humanity becomes victimized by shame and disgrace. The casualties are everywhere: our friends, family members, coworkers, strangers—and dare I say—us.

Right now, take some time and think about this past week.

How often did you walk the busy halls or walkways, feeling the stabbing ache of complete loneliness or rejection? When you last stepped into a church, was there any part of you that felt fake, worthless, or inadequate? At your latest meal with friends, did you question yourself about whether you measured up to the guys or girls—the men or women—around you? Or were there moments when bitterness and envy surfaced at the most inappropriate times?

An interesting study has found that under the thick layers of all of these feelings and emotions resides the heaviness of shame. In short, shame is what consistently explains why we feel alone, fake, worthless, inadequate, envious, inferior, or bitter.

"Because I deserve this, I am not good enough," it whispers.

Author Lewis Smedes defines shame in this way:

"The feeling of shame is about our very *selves*—not
about some bad thing we *did* or *said* but about what
we are. It tells us that we *are* unworthy."

It is this deep feeling of unworthiness or "missing the mark" that
relates us to the lepers written about in scripture. They were, to sum
it up, scum in their society.

According to Jewish law, when a person began showing signs
of leprosy, the city was to literally dispose of him or her. In fact,
surrounding most big cities of the day were leper colonies, groups of
suffering people forced to live a life of seclusion and shame.

And no one fought for the justice and health of a leper.

Why? Because leprosy was nasty. Not only was it completely
contagious, but it was also undoubtedly deadly. Imagine sores, boils,
and flaky white scales forming all over your body. And as the disease
progressed, it would begin deteriorating both your muscles and your
bones. As you can imagine, this was a slow, painful, and brutally
embarrassing process.

Often the pain would become so unbearable that lepers would
seek other means toward death. And if that doesn't sound bad enough,
then understand this: Society regarded this disease as a plague from
God, punishing certain people for their certainly terrible sins. To
everyone else, leprosy was God's outward showing of his hate for
the leper.

Naturally, this brought lepers a few steps down on the totem pole
of "who's who" in Jewish culture. It didn't matter who you once were,
the name you once had, or the reputation you once bore—because
all of it vanished the second the sores began to form. So not only did
they feel the constant pain of leprosy, but also the deep ache of being
different and *hated* by their people and their God.

In order for "healthy and righteous" citizens to avoid a run-in with a leper, the infected were instructed to always make known that they were close by. Instead of being commanded to call out something as simple as *leprosy* or *sick*, they were instructed to scream aloud the word *"unclean."*

In fact, lepers were forbidden to step foot in a public place without yelling it over and over and over, making sure that people had enough time to dodge any contact with them. This simple yet degrading law made a leper's vocabulary quite limited.

Imagine the brokenness of having to constantly make known your deepest pain. Without a doubt, this law allowed their full identity to be shaped around this overly spoken word. And with it came shame, disgrace, isolation, and hopelessness.

This new "name" led them to the belief that they were all alone and deserved it. Like every victim of shame, they soon lost their ability to separate their present condition from the overall view they had of themselves. Regardless of what they once were—a son, daughter, loved, or beautiful—they were now indoctrinated with the title of being impure, polluted, tainted, and filthy.

Unlike an adulterous woman or petty thief in their day, everyone knew exactly where a leper was and exactly who they were; *unclean.*

BRINGING IT HOME

So where is the comparison? you may ask. Like many truths, it is hidden deep beneath the painful layers of both you and the leper. No, we do not have painful sores that deteriorate much of our bodies. And no, we do not have to walk around screaming aloud the very word that we fear defines us—thankfully so.

But regardless of what society saw of them or what punishment seemed to be placed in their lives, at their core, all lepers had a human heart broken by shame-filled lies. Like many of us, the humanness of these lepers felt every bit of scorn thrown at them by the world. They were men and women, made in God's image, who slowly bought into the lie that they were unlovable.

Is this not true for us as well? We, too, are God's beautiful creation. And we, too, have hearts that are deeply hurt by the world around us.

It is seen and felt daily.

It is in the eyes of those who pass us by, on the billboards that flaunt everything we do not have, and in the mirror as we stare at what we do not like. Our minds are constantly saturated with negative thoughts and ideas that are not our own.

They are lies formed specifically for us from our enemy. Even though they may seem harmless, they both directly and indirectly war against the truth of who we are in God's sight.

Starting at birth, these lies erupt in our hearts and become our *norm*. They impact the actions that we choose to make, only resulting in more shame. And the saddest thing of all is how deep and true they have become to us. Personally, I am amazed at how natural it is for me to dismiss truth by filling my head with an orchestra of negative thoughts.

And every maturing believer knows the pain of these lies.

They creep up at the most inopportune time, telling us that we are not good enough. They overwhelm us during the night, making it nearly impossible to fall back asleep. They come into our prayer lives, distracting us from ever forming a real prayer. They cloud our experience of joy, peace, and comfort, and they keep us from being completely honest with the body of believers that surrounds us.

I was reminded of this while talking with a close friend.

For eight years of her life, she struggled deeply with pornography. Yes, *she*. And like all addictions, its power seemed unbreakable. "The most shameful part," she said, "was how ugly and alone it made me feel."

And this makes sense. Being in a world where pornography tends to be communicated as a male issue, no wonder a woman would feel isolated. Her sin was in the dark. And in the dark, lies were spoken.

Although she has experienced the Lord's freedom from this sin, it is clear that the enemy's lies have tried to keep both the pain and shame of it alive. Over coffee, she let me hear a few of the phrases that still creep up in her day:

> *I have to do something better.*
> *I have to be something better.*
> *I am a failure.*
> *My heart will never be completely healed.*
> *I will never be loved.*
> *I have too many issues.*
> *I should just give up.*

At times she believes these words are true; that they are the result of the sins that she committed and that she deserves every one of them. Even though she knows of her newness in Christ Jesus, these lies still war at her daily.

And as they were flowing from her mouth, I was hit with the realization that I, too, tend to believe these same words. In fact, these are just a few of the lies our hearts believe. If we are honest, we could each add a few of our own to this list.

But each phrase is directly from our enemy.

Much like a leper's lie, they each tell us that we are alone. And much like a leper's lie, they try to make us believe that who we are is shameful and unclean.

THE FIGHT WITH SHAME

For those of us who are familiar with Mark's version of the leper's story, we know that not every person in Galilee chose to see this man as forever unclean.

Mark writes it eloquently:

> And a leper came to Jesus, beseeching Him and falling on his knees before Him, and saying, "If You are willing, You can make me clean." Moved with compassion, Jesus stretched out His hand and touched him, and said to him, "I am willing; be cleansed." Immediately the leprosy left him and he was cleansed.
>
> -Mark 1:40-42

These three verses are incredibly beautiful. No matter how unclean this man was and how shameful he felt, he was not too much for the precious love of Christ Jesus.

And this is profound.

His problems were not bigger than the love and power of Jesus.

I imagine that for weeks he had heard talk concerning this Jesus of Nazareth, a man who claimed to be the Messiah. In the midst of this leper shouting and feeling shame, he somehow stopped and heard the truth of a man who had the power to make all things clean.

As this happened, he slowly began experiencing something unheard of for a leper: hope. A part of me wonders how long it took for this hope to build in him the confidence to face this man, Jesus.

But confident he soon became.

Being a leper, he was commanded to never speak anything but "unclean." However, here we see him stating a whole sentence: "If You are willing, You can make me clean."

This in itself was a huge leap of faith.

And no one could have guessed what happened next.

Jesus Christ—the Rabbi, the good teacher—was spoken to by a disgusting and dirty leper. A scenario like this should never have happened. But in one instance, this man was heard, looked upon with eyes of compassion, spoken to, and touched by Christ.

These are four things that no leper on earth understood or experienced—*ever*.

He was *heard, looked at, spoken to*, and *touched*.

Immediately, in the blink of an eye, he was cleansed. Every ounce of the disease was gone. What a miracle!

Although this is truly amazing, it does not even come close to what Jesus really did for him. You see, during these four things, something completely glorious was communicated and made real for the leper.

It was this: *Jesus was willing*.

"If You are willing, You can make me clean," he says. In other words: "If You think I am worth it... If You are willing to see me as enough... If You see something in me... If You want to spend your time on me... You can make me clean."

And as I said, Jesus was willing.

In the presence of the willing Messiah, all of the shameful lies that he believed about himself were silenced. For once, someone saw him as more than a leper.

That day, he became clean.

That day, he became new, holy, and righteous.

You see, the cleansing power of Jesus is shame-killing. As believers, we know this as a fact. Like this leper, we have been made new, holy, and righteous through Christ.

Although this is true, we are surrounded by a world full of our old life. A world that painstakingly reminds us of the habits that were once consuming, the false beliefs that were once binding, and our old ruler who shames us toward believing that all of it is still true.

He is there, in the shadows of our day, pointing out the reminders of our past, calling forward our deep insecurities, and pressuring us to take them back.

Take a moment and ponder this: "If I am truly righteous, why do I believe that I am _____?" Fill in the blank with your shameful lie: insignificant, worthless, ugly, disgusting, unlovable, alone, controlled by my sins, or defined by my past.

Believe it or not, we all struggle with these lies.

But the life of shame is a complete threat to our life of holiness. No, it has no power over us; but yes, it can halt us in our pursuit of obeying Christ. Because of this, the shame-filled lies that are whispered to us daily need to be dealt with. And the enemy, the father of these false words, needs to be silenced.

My friend said it perfectly:

I knew that I was righteous. I knew that Jesus redeemed my heart...
But what I needed was a redeemed mind.

With that said, I challenge you to begin a journey with me as we dive deep into our hearts, uncover our shameful lies, and redeem the way that we see both ourselves and our Lord.

For we are not shameful when found in Christ.

Much like the "unclean" man's journey to Jesus, this will require us to take chances through faith. And the exciting thing is that we already know the ending. Like the cleansed leper, Jesus is willing. And in His presence, we will be heard, looked upon, spoken to, and touched.

The unashamed life starts now.

QUESTIONS FOR REFLECTION

1. Can you relate to the story of the leper? If yes, in what way?

2. Look back at the "believed lies" listed in this chapter. Which one(s) do you feel like are your own?

3. "If I am truly righteous, why do I believe that I am_____?" *Challenge yourself to honestly fill in this blank.

4. Where you are now, do you genuinely think that your feelings of shame will ever end? Why or why not?

CHAPTER 2

HEALTHY SHAME

Woe is me, for I am ruined! Because I am a
man of unclean lips, And I live among people
of unclean lips; For my eyes have seen
the King, the LORD of hosts.
-Isaiah 6:5

Although I completely hate to admit it, I am not, in any way, a genius.

It's true. And I came to this conclusion very early on in my life. When I was younger, let's say around ten, I found complete joy while playing with random chemicals.

Yes, chemicals.

It all began when I got this awesome science set for my birthday. Laugh if you will, but this gift was amazing. It included a microscope, dissection equipment, and about fifteen containers of chemicals that were labeled "toxic."

To a ten year old boy, toxic meant *awesome*.

For days, I would mix these liquids together and dump my finished concoction onto anything that was close. Nothing was safe from my wrath. Any nearby plastics, woods, and metals soon became doused. After a few less than adequate attempts, I decided that my mixture needed a little extra kick. So naturally I found myself in our garage collecting every liquid in sight.

I quickly got what I needed and went to my "laboratory." Under the protection of my wooden fort, I began my new experiments. My mission was simple: mix them all.

Sadly, this ended rather quickly when my glass cylinder tipped over, spilling the mixture onto my fort. In the matter of seconds, I discovered that I had invented an acid that could eat through wood. Even though I am not a genius, I feel as if I should receive some type of medal for this discovery.

But before you begin to worry, know that neither animal nor person was harmed during this experiment. My fort, on the other hand, had a wonderful hollowed-out spot on it.

I would like to say that this instilled fear and caused me to halt what I was doing, but that would be a lie. I neglected the warning this acid gave me. Even though this is true, in hindsight, I did learn something: there is a huge value in *understanding*.

Looking back, I probably should not have played with random liquids so blindly. I could have definitely poisoned myself. The mystery of my experiments was alluring, but I realized quickly that *blindness is rarely beneficial*. You see, without understanding, it is hard to produce healthy growth.

And this same lesson can be applied to silencing Satan and ending our battle with shame. In any given day, we can come across a number of different types of shame. Although it may be surprising, not all shame is at war with our spiritual lives; and not all shame should be labeled as toxic.

But if we continue to live blindly, we will never distinguish the differences between healthy and unhealthy shame. As you can imagine, this can really hurt the growth of our relationship with Jesus.

Without a doubt, I could have easily continued to blindly mix liquids on my fort. In fact, I could have continued it all the way to the present day. But now that I am much older, people would begin to question why an adult is acting like a child; why an adult lacks that significant growth.

If we want our lives to mature in the Lord, then our understanding must mature as well. For shame cannot be battled unless we are first made aware of its many aspects.

GUILT AND SHAME

With that said, I want you to pause and ask yourself this question: *Is there a difference between guilt and shame?*

Is there?

And if so, what is it? Is shame just guilt in **bolded**, ALL-CAPPED letters? Can they be used interchangeably? Is one good and the other bad? Or do they have separate meanings that evoke completely different emotions?

Over the years, many researchers have taken these questions to the streets in order to see how the average person would answer them. As you can imagine, the results continually revealed that people's answers are all across the board.

The fact is that most people do not know of the important distinction between these two words. You see, guilt is being *in the wrong*, while shame is the belief that *you are the wrong.*

We feel guilty about what we do and we feel shame for who we are.

Guilt is accompanied with actions and behavior, while shame deals heavily with our overall beliefs about how our actions and behavior relate to ourselves. To some extent, guilt and shame have the ability to either bring repentance or bind us completely from it.

A healthy dose of each is rather normal for our spiritual lives, while too much can become overwhelming and overcoming for anyone. Although they may work together, they are in no way one. In many cases, guilt is the avenue to shame.

And we have all experienced this transition.

When I moved from middle school to high school, many things changed in my life. For one, I finally moved out of that awkward stage in life. Clothes started fitting properly, my voice finally dropped, and I was finally getting armpit hair (which is a big deal for a boy, trust me). But sadly, this new stage also brought me to a place of experiencing both guilt and shame.

Friends started to change, parties became the norm of life, and girls quickly grabbed my attention.

In this new world, there were so many temptations that seemed to distract me and lure me toward sin. And soon, I caved. The things that I began doing were in direct conflict with who I was and who I proclaimed to be. Even though I was a Bible-reading Christian, my hidden actions did not show it.

Naturally, I felt a heavy sense of guilt for my behaviors. I hated what I was doing, and I felt it every Sunday and Wednesday night. But the guilt and shame distinction came when my struggles became consuming and defining.

As time passed, I began believing the lie that I was my sin.

It was this moment where my guilty behavior transitioned into a shameful heart that felt alone, worthless, and disgusting. My perception shifted from me hating my actions, to me also hating myself. And like many others who have fallen into this trap, my regret and strong sense of guilt led to a shameful heart.

Guilt and shame are completely different.

Completely.

THE GOOD KIND OF "FEELING BAD"

As confusing as it may sound, there is a good kind of "feeling bad" in the Christian life; a good type of shame. Unlike negative shame, this feeling is very normal for us as created beings.

It is what makes us human.

In fact, healthy shame positions our hearts toward our Creator. This shame is not the weighed down belief of being completely alone, unworthy, and nothing, but the balanced and humble perception of who we are in light of how *great* God is.

Where negative shame is a lie from the devil, healthy shame is a truth from the Holy Spirit within us. Satan points a finger at us, saying "YOU are worthless and shameful," while the Spirit points a finger at Himself, the Triune God, saying "I am GREAT. And nothing compares to Me."

Do you see the difference? It's a huge perspective change. And this healthy and moderate sense of shame is very beneficial to both our private and collective spiritual journeys.

Just take a look at the life of Isaiah.

In chapter 6 of his book, Isaiah writes of a vision that he had, one ending in these words:

> Woe is me, for I am *ruined!* Because I am a man of
> unclean lips, And I live among people of unclean lips;
> For my eyes have seen the King, the LORD of hosts.
> -Isaiah 6:5

What would it be like to *see* the Lord in heaven; to literally see Him on His throne, high and exalted; with His glory completely filling the vast room that you are in?

Everywhere you look would be God.

If you can, imagine the beauty that would surround you. Feel the fear in seeing heavenly guards, creatures that your eyes have never looked upon before, and hearing them *scream* aloud praises to their Lord. Their voices proclaiming the exact truth of what is before you:

> Holy, Holy, Holy, is the LORD of hosts, The whole earth is full of His glory.
>
> -Isaiah 6:3

Then, as if this is not already overwhelming enough, the ground begins to shake at the sound of *His* voice (6:4-5). Yes, His voice brings about an earthquake. The very temple walls are trembling as resonant tones vibrate and spread throughout. Without a doubt, you would begin to shake with holy terror.

But that's not all. Suddenly, smoke starts rising, becoming the only thing that you can see. Your senses are completely overtaken. Yet it is at this very moment that all of us, every single one of us, would fall to the floor and say a phrase very similar to Isaiah's:

"I am nothing! Because I am a man of unclean lips, and I live among people of unclean lips!"

And there it would be.

The real life experience of *healthy* shame.

We are Nothing

Healthy shame is found in the appropriate amount of humanness we feel in light of God's glory. All of Isaiah's senses were being engulfed in the splendor, the wonder, and the sheer magnitude of who God is. And it was through seeing "the King, the Lord of hosts" that he felt shame.

This, however, is not the all-encompassing feeling of nothingness found in unhealthy shame, but the feeling of being nothing *only* in relation to God. As believers, our healthy shame enables us to see the Lord and communicate to Him. When we grow in the knowledge of just how great He is, our only response is to be humbled by what we discover and to submit to Him in worship.

We can understand this level of healthy shame when focusing on our astonishment with great things. A sunset across rushing tides, the foggy depth of the Grand Canyon, the grandeur of the night sky, or the beauty of a natural forest.

If you are like me, then these things amaze you. For being in the presence of something so grand shows us just how small we are. But more importantly, our God made these things; He literally *spoke* them into reality. Because of this, these sights give us glimpses of His majesty.

In light of Him, we are small.

Woe are we in comparison to the magnificence of our God.

I know it may not seem like it, but this mind-set, the mind-set of being *nothing* in comparison to the LORD of hosts, is worship. Isaiah saw God's beauty, and his response of humility rang out as true worship. No, he did not burst into song or chant, but he did reply to God's presence with a heart posture of surrender.

A falling on his face kind of surrender.

Healthy shame reminds us of who God is and positions our hearts toward responding to Him with everything we have.

We See Our Sins

But it does not stop here.

Healthy shame not only reminds us that we are nothing in relation to God, a true sign of worship, but also allows us to see our sin; that we are "a man of unclean lips." (6:5)

When saying this, Isaiah could have meant a multitude of different things. Whether he is talking about a specific situation or general lifestyle that he was living, one thing is for certain: he recognized and confessed his sin.

And it comes out quickly.

Paul states that our words are an overflow of our heart. In this instance, Isaiah recognized that the posture of his heart had been in conflict with God. The humility of being in the presence of the Lord is what led him to become dissatisfied with his actions. It allowed him to see his sin as sin.

Although this is true, I must make an important distinction. Before this encounter with God, Isaiah was *defined* by his sin. In today's world, this vision could be seen as the moment of Isaiah's *salvation*, although this concept is mostly used in the New Testament.

And salvation or *atonement* is what Isaiah discovered.

> Then one of the seraphs [angels] flew to me with a live coal in his hand, which he had taken with tongs from the altar. With it he touched my mouth and said, "See, this has touched your lips; your guilt is taken away and your sin atoned for."
>
> -Isaiah 6:6-7

Through the burning of this coal, Isaiah's guilt and sinfulness—or dare we say, shame—was completely cleansed. Here we see that Isaiah's experience of healthy shame changed his reality of negative shame. And it was through this that Isaiah realized his purpose and new life in the Lord.

Much like Isaiah, we have had this cleansing experience. I imagine that not many of them involved hot coals, but it is true to say that all of them involved guilt being "taken away" and "sin atoned for." Because of that, healthy shame does not remind us that we are *sinners*, that's the lie of unhealthy shame. Instead, it points out the sin that we still choose to commit, reminding us that it is not who we are; that it is not who we are called to be.

Lewis Smedes states it this way:

> "A creature meant to be a little less than God is likely to feel a deep dissatisfaction with herself if she falls a notch below the splendid human being she is meant to be. If we never feel shame, we may have lost contact with the person we most truly are."

Because we are new creations, healthy shame does not tell us that we are sinful, but shows us that we are not acting like the splendid, beautiful, and new creatures that we truly are in Christ. It is through this shame that we can realize our sins and remind ourselves that we are called to be set free from them.

We Can Confidently Act

Through Isaiah's shame, we now understand that he was able to see, communicate, and worship the Lord of hosts. Quickly this led to him discovering and confessing the sin in his heart. As readers, we can see the beautiful shift in his life. But what happened next is something that naturally occurs when God powerfully transforms a heart.

Isaiah *confidently acted*. For the surrender found in healthy shame always leads to action.

Then I heard the voice of the Lord, saying, "Whom shall I send, and who will go for Us?" Then I said, "Here am I. Send me!"

-Isaiah 6:8

When the Lord's presence humbles our hearts, we are able to both hear His commands and confidently obey them. Here, we see that Isaiah's reverence and humility did not make him timid or insecure.

Instead, being in this state of healthy shame, Isaiah had a clear picture of who God was and who he, himself, was. Here in the Lord's presence, Isaiah boldly steps out and acts. You see, obedience seems quite natural during those times when we feel most overcome with His presence.

Think about it.

The last time that you felt alive in God's presence—whether at a worship service, a church camp, alone with a best friend, or lying in your bed by yourself—were you not ready to do whatever it was that the Lord asked of you?

The funny thing is that during these times, we do not even think about if we are actually "the ones" for the job. His presence both around us and inside of us stirs up a strong boldness and confidence.

This is why you stood up in that worship service, submitting your life to missions; why you walked down to the front altar to pray over a brokenhearted brother or sister; or why you spoke loving, yet bold truth to a dear friend.

In each instance, we confidently and obediently acted.

And this is what God desires from us. Much like Isaiah, a healthy shame humbles us toward true dependence on God. And this dependence goes hand in hand with the surrender needed to obey.

But sadly, life is full of valleys; full of times when the healthy shame of surrender and action becomes dry and passive. It is here where Satan steps up to take a swing at us with his shame.

The Shift

I have chosen to begin with this view of shame because I want your heart to be well acquainted with it as you continue on. In fact, this is the last time that we will speak directly of healthy shame. But know this: negative shame can only be beaten through the consistent exposure of God's presence. Soon you will discover this more and more.

My prayer right now is that you may grow deeper in the knowledge of who God is, so that through healthy shame, your heart can continually worship, confess, and confidently obey His call on your life. The battle through shame takes determination. But with God's help, it can end.

QUESTIONS FOR REFLECTION

1. When looking back on your life, how has your guilt morphed into shame?

2. Have you ever experienced a "Woe is me" moment like Isaiah? If so, write it out.

3. Is there something that you have been called to "confidently act" on? How can you pursue that?

4. When approaching your negative shame, how can you constantly practice healthy shame?

CHAPTER 3

UNHEALTHY SHAME

*"You can find shame in every house,
burning in an ashtray, hanging
framed upon a wall, covering a bed.
But nobody notices it anymore."*
-Salman Rushdie

*"Mine has been a life of much shame.
I can't even guess what it must be to live
the life of a human being."*
-Osamu Dazai

If healthy shame plays a large role in our connection to God, then it seems pretty obvious for *negative shame* to do the complete opposite. One shows us our need and dependence on God, drawing us closer to Him, while the other distorts our view of both ourselves and God, turning us further away from Him.

This image of "turning away" will be seen perfectly in Chapter 6 where we will discuss the very beginning of shame. But before that, we must first do some pre-work: *How does negative shame begin? Who is it communicated by? And what all does it do?*

The Beginning Lie of Shame

Shame exposes itself in a multitude of ways. It is in the quiet, polite, yet insecure girl who is everyone's friend; in the obnoxious frat boy who tries to convince everyone—and himself—that his life is awesome; in the over-achieving father who works hard to both provide for his family and hide his secret life; and in the typical "good guy," plagued with the horrors and decisions of his past.

Each example is so different, yet each example portrays the same deep shame. So I will say it again; *shame exposes itself in a multitude of ways*. Because of this, we have a tendency to overlook the common threads that tie every one of these stories, and every one of *our* stories, together. You see, when dealing with shame, two things are always at play: one, it began from a deeply believed lie, and two, it is a direct attack on our *whole self*.

In fact, this type of shame is completely rooted in deceit, meaning that its growth is dependent on the depth of the lie believed. Once implanted in us, this shameful lie aims at distorting our perception of everything around us and everything inside of us. Before we know it, our whole world seems to be under attack. Although this sounds easy to wrap our minds around, shame is actually very complicated.

In 1994, Walt Disney Pictures released *the best-ever* animated musical drama: *The Lion King* (Yes…the best-ever). Within a few short weeks, the popularity of this film spread like wildfire. Everybody was humming the tunes and walking around with their very own Simba t-shirt. Even today, it is hard to find someone who has seen this childhood classic and did not enjoy every second of it.

If you cannot tell, I was and am still a complete fan (I had the bed set and all).

But it was not just the catchy music that grabbed the world's attention. In fact, the story line itself is a heart-throbbing hook for all viewers. It portrays a young, runaway cub who returns home in order to save the animal kingdom from complete destruction. Although it is not the main aspect of this film, I am stunned by how wonderfully it displays the journey and overall battle of shame.

Before Simba, the hero of the film, runs away, he faces something extremely devastating. While playing with a friend, Simba is met by an oncoming stampede. Out of nowhere, Mufasa, Simba's father, races on the scene to rescue his son.

Although the save was successful, his father is left hanging from a cliff above the stampede. And up comes Scar, Mufasa's jealous brother. In an attempt to get rid of Mufasa, Scar lets his own brother fall into the roaring stampede below.

When everything is clear and all the animals are out of sight, you see a brokenhearted Simba trying to wake up his father. The scene depicts a clear picture of how easy it is for our judgment to get clouded when we are vulnerable. As Simba is grieving, Scar approaches from the distance. Instead of comforting his own nephew, He plants a lie deep within Simba's heart: "**YOU** killed the King," he exclaims, "**YOU** are a murderer."

As this lie begins to take root in Simba, you can see the work of shame in his face. Scar tells him that the best thing to do is run away, seeing as he is too much of a "disgrace" to stay.

"Run away and *never* return!"

And Simba does just that. He runs as fast as he can, leaving behind everything that he knew as home.

The saddest part of this whole scene is that innocent Simba began believing that he was a murderer. As the viewer, we know that it was Scar who actually murdered Mufasa, the King. And in an attempt to rule the kingdom himself, Scar chose to impose this heavy lie in Simba's heart, sending him, the only other heir, far away.

But the moment that Simba believed that he was to blame was the moment that his heart became bound by undeserved shame.

THE "WHO" OF NEGATIVE SHAME

Because the seed of negative shame is always a lie, it seems natural to wonder the "how" and "who" of a lie. Like any form of communication, lies can be heard either directly or indirectly.

The lie that Scar imposes upon Simba is a perfect example of one that is direct: "**YOU** killed the King!" These are the verbal lies that seemed to be aimed directly at us word for word. Although they are first spoken to us from an outside voice, they quickly latch themselves onto our mind's inner whisper.

Most of the time, these words stem from the mouths of those closest to us. Without meaning to, an innocent phrase can become a shame-filled tune. In a conversation with a small group of freshmen guys, I was reminded of how often our fathers can be the source of that innocent phrase.

After a difficult day at school, one of the guys approached his father. "Hey Dad, I bet I could take you down!" he said playfully. In hearing this challenge, his dad looked up from his reading and quickly remarked: "There is no way. Look at how small you are!"

And in an instant, a lie was heard.

The crazy thing is that the retelling of this story, or should I say, the *first* telling of this story, occurred eight years after the fact. So for eight long years, this boy held onto the lie that he was "small," "minimal," and "not good enough." As you can imagine, his inner voice picked up that vocabulary and expanded it over time.

But that is just one of the millions of examples.

The second type of communicated lies are those that are indirect. These are covertly hidden in our day. It is through the continual exposure of these fallacies that shame begins to grow. They come from the images, words, and expressions that we see and hear on the TV screen, in social media, at our schools, at work, and in our homes.

Most often, they are ideas or views expressed by the world around us that, over time, become etched inside of our own minds as the truth or "the norm."

A perfect example of this is through looking at the impact that media plays in our hearts. On a daily basis, television and social media *speak* to us, telling us what is most desired by the world. We hear over and over that in order to be heard, to be wanted, or to be successful, *this* must happen or we must wear *that*. Unlike direct lies, these seem to make it into our hearts without us ever realizing them.

In fact, a recent study showed that social media is now one of the leading causes of self-esteem issues among teenagers and young adults. *Why?* It is because throughout social media you see a common thread of "virtual perfection."

Think about it. If you scan a news feed, you cannot help but see this in action: people only posting "the cutest" pictures of themselves, only submitting things that make their lives sound more pleasurable and desirable, and only letting viewers in on the "ideal" side of who they are. This "virtual perfection," when seen over and over, communicates so many shameful lies to every viewer who clearly cannot match what they constantly see.

And because these lies are woven inside the world around us, they are the hardest to separate from truth. And before we know it, we can begin to feel bound by the shame that accompanies them. Once a lie is planted and the roots go deep, shame can grow and grow.

Even though these lies, both direct and indirect, are communicated to us by the physical world around us, there is something deeply spiritual about them. In fact, every bit of the physical world around us is ruled by a spiritual being. Although this is a hard concept to grasp, the Bible tells us that there is a *ruler of this world* who constantly seeks to own everything in it.

As believers, we know of this person as our ultimate enemy, someone who is given the title of the "Father of lies." Because of this, it seems pretty obvious that every lie created and communicated, although spoken to us by real people, is actually first issued by this ultimate liar.

Satan, the enemy, seeks to rule this world through making us believe his words. Although this is true, he can no longer rule us, for we are followers of the one, true Lord. We are unable to serve two masters and Satan knows this.

Therefore, his strategy with us is much like Scar's strategy with Simba: *plant a lie deep within our hearts,* however small it may be. For he knows that once it is believed, it can cause us to run far from the person we are, the Kingdom that is all around us, and the work that we are destined to do.

As we will soon uncover in Chapter 4, Satan can *only* plant the lies within us, leaving us responsible for the beliefs and actions that may follow. But first, what "fruit" does this shameful lie have the possibility of growing?

Shame Attacks our Identity

Our enemy *knows* who we are.

Although we constantly doubt and question our new identity in Christ, it is a foundational truth that Satan knows for certain. When he sees us, he sees a completely new and forgiven person. Because of this, he does not doubt the true power that comes with who we are.

This is why Satan tries so hard to distract us from this truth. With every lie comes the hope that we will dismiss our newness; that we will focus on his false creation of who we are and miss the reality. Although they start off subtle, these lies have the potential to change the perception that we have about ourselves.

Instead of a clay jar holding a never ending treasure, we begin to only focus on the messy, scratched up, and cracked outer clay.

And this is done through morphing a lie into shame.

This is where Scar's words of "You killed the King" transitions into Simba's words of "I killed the King." And as this lie festers, an identity is formed: "I am a murderer; a disgrace." And before Simba knew it, his heart became deeply ashamed.

This shame is what carried him through the next few years of his life, shaping him into something very different than he once was. In fact, he completely left behind his princehood. As the story continues, we find that as Simba grows, so does his shame. It becomes a lens through which he begins to see the whole world.

Fear, anxiety, a low sense of self-worth, and an even lower sense of potential accompanies a shameful lens.

Much like Simba, the deep lies communicated by Satan can cause us to shape our lives around being a person that is everything *but* who we were created to be. Because he cannot control us, he wants to bring to life a shameful lie that we choose to feed. And over time, this imposed shame changes us, covering up our overall ability to see who we really are.

Where healthy shame points us more and more to self-discovery, negative shame turns us further away from it.

In fact, Satan hopes to shame us to the point that we choose to leave behind the identity that we have. His desire is that we "run away and never return." And as we embark on a journey away from God's grace, we begin to comprehend all things through that dark lens.

Shame Attacks our Kingdom

Whether or not you have realized this, *you*, in Christ, have become *one* with both Him and every human being that is also found in Him. This is why the Church, the *real* church, is called the united "Body of Christ."

In the letter to the Church in Ephesus, Paul urges them to realize that they (plural) are actually *one* (singular). You see, as a body they were being hit hard with disunity. Therefore, Paul states over and over and over that the church and every member in it makes up the *fullness of God* (1:22-23).

As believers and heirs in Christ's Kingdom, we literally make up His body. This means that when we all are united together, His *fullness* is seen and expressed. This is why Paul urges so many of the early church members to be united, so that Christ can be seen and glorified.

Satan, on the other hand, does not have this same desire.

In fact, he wants nothing to do with the unity and fullness of Christ. James writes that God's oneness actually makes the demons *shudder* in fear. Satan literally trembles when we, as Christ's body, are most unified. So in order to stop this, he aims at separating us and distorting that unity.

If he can break us apart, then he can once again regain that lost traction in our hearts and minds; he can "turn the volume up" on his personal microphone.

In *The Lion King*, Scar knew that regardless of what lie Simba believed, that his family and kingdom would constantly be there for him. Because of this, Scar aimed at preventing Simba from ever being in true contact with them again. For if Simba did return home, Scar knew that he would be welcomed back with open arms (or paws).

But Simba's growing feeling of shame made this fact seem very unrealistic. Since he could not live with what he thought he had done, he believed that *no one else could either*. Because of this, he ran far away, leaving behind the very community that would help him heal.

His shame led him straight toward isolation.

And this is true for us. If Satan can lead us into shame, he can draw us away from the community that is around us. He knows that true freedom comes from us being in unity with both the Spirit and other believers. So in an effort to bind us to shame, he sends us running away from the Body, scared to ever return.

This is why we, as Christians, feel so alone and unheard.

And if you are honest with yourself, you can clearly see this play out in your own life. When you feel shame, guilt, and regret, your gut reaction is to retreat from the people who love you. You fear that they will judge you when they see you for who you truly are, or that they will not be able to understand and sympathize with your pain.

Too often, we believe that we are alone.

But in reality, we are never truly alone; we are forever *one* with Jesus and His people. Our shame, however, has shifted our perception, causing us to believe that in order to stay safe or protected, we must run away. This does not mean that we literally sprint at the sight of human contact. But in our shame we build up walls, we construct strongholds, and we place dozens of inner barriers.

Once these are present, they prevent us from being sincerely honest, open, and vulnerable with the Body of which we are a part.

Our shame leads us straight toward isolation.

Shame Attacks our Purpose

In the midst of losing sight of both our identity and our Kingdom, Satan also targets our purpose. In the same letter to the Ephesians, Paul writes a prayer that he had for them:

> I pray that the eyes of your heart may be enlightened
> in order that you may know the hope to which He
> has called you, the riches of His glorious inheritance
> in the saints, and the incomparably great power for
> us who believe.
>
> -Ephesians 1:18-19

In these verses, Paul prays that the people of this church would realize their purpose. He desires for them to *know* their calling and the inheritance and power that comes with it. Because above all, Paul knew that they were called and given the purpose of obeying God and ruling *with* Him.

And as Simba ran away from both who he was and the kingdom to which he belonged, he also ran away from his purpose. He was next in line to lead his people; he was the *heir* to the throne. But this truth was clouded when he was in the epicenter of shame.

The only thing that was on his mind was doing exactly what the liar told him to do. Everything else seemed to be a blur. His focus was tainted as he allowed the shame to take hold of his heart and mind. It had broken him in a way that seemed unmendable.

And as the years passed, you can see how shame made his heart harden: "Hakuna Matata, what a wonderful phrase...."

As you may know, this "wonderful" phrase is centered on having *no worries*. So in order to lessen the pain and dissatisfaction erupting in his heart, Simba quickly bought into this idea.

While he was off living a numb life with "no worries," Scar had turned his homeland into a place of suffering and bondage. But his feelings of shame clouded this, allowing him to leave behind his kingship and his responsibilities. This decision neglected the hurting animal kingdom at large.

Shame in its deepest form leads to a heavy passivity and numbness. These feelings, above all, will point us away from the eternal purpose that we have in obeying God. If we believe that we are *unlovable* and have *no one who truly loves us*, then our next step is to feel like we have no *meaning* or *calling*.

Just like Simba, we will naturally latch onto worldly things and ideas that seem to lessen our pain, delivering us over to the feeling of numbness and passivity. A Christian who is numb, dry, and fruitless is a Christian hiding the felt shame and pain of their past. And if Satan can push us toward this, he can prevent us from doing the work that we were designed to do.

In our shame, we become numb; and in our numbness, we become purposeless.

It Hurts, Right?

Because shame tends to become our norm, this chapter may be the first time you have ever realized the depth of your own shame; and this realization may hurt. No one wants to realize that their shame is the very reason that they are missing out on their identity, their community, or their purpose in life.

Although this is true, please realize that you have just begun this book. You may feel the weight of your shame now, but your journey toward battling it is still ongoing and active.

Awareness is always the first step. And even though it is tough, it is through awareness that we can find change.

There is more to learn and more to uncover; especially about our enemy.

QUESTIONS FOR REFLECTION

1. What are some direct and indirect lies that you hear daily?

2. Have any of these lies made you reshape your view of yourself?

3. Who are some people that your shame has isolated you from?

4. In ending this chapter, write out what you are experiencing, thinking, feeling, etc. Let these few sentences be genuine, raw, and vulnerable.

CHAPTER 4

THE "SHAMER" AND HIS TACTICS

*"By mixing a little truth, the enemy
had made his lie far stronger."*
- C.S. Lewis

*"The devil is no idle spirit, but a vagrant,
runagate walker, that never rests in one place.
The motive, cause, and main intention of his
walking is to ruin man."*
-Thomas Adams

My wedding day is one that I will never forget.

Without a doubt, it is one of most beautiful moments I have ever experienced. All morning and afternoon, I was the crazy one running around and micromanaging everyone in sight while my bride-to-be was off getting pampered.

As you can tell, I am still a little jealous.

The hardest thing was to just sit in that back room and wait for the ceremony to begin. I kept finding myself checking the time. My heart constantly pounded as the clock never seemed to move.

But finally, four o'clock came.

As I stood up front, my knees were quivering and shaking; I was so ready to see her. The cello was playing, all of my closest friends were walking in, and then, without missing a beat, there she was.

She was perfect, beautiful, and blameless.

My eyes, now soggy with tears, could not look away.

Although the rest of the ceremony is a blur, there is one thing that I will never forget. As we stood up there on that stage, I had complete confidence in who God made me to be. I can remember looking into her eyes and *knowing* that I was created to be with her; that she is my beloved and I am hers.

In that moment, I felt God's presence very tangibly.

And in that moment, I felt His blessing.

This was truly incredible, but in no way did it prepare me for what was to come. Although I have fought plenty of spiritual battles in my lifetime, none can compare with what I came up against that evening. The stresses, excitement, and overall emotions of the day wore me out, leaving me extremely vulnerable to the enemy's attacks.

And on the car ride to our hotel, the lies began.

"You don't deserve her. I mean, look at her beauty. You know what you have done in the past…the acts that you've committed. Do you think that she will truly love you, the *real* you?"

As I sat there and listened, my mind replayed every sexual act that I had ever experienced or initiated in my life. Each of them were aspects of my past; ones that I had already confessed and received healing from. But in this moment, they felt present once again, filling me with guilt, regret, and an intense shame.

Although my wife knew every bit of my story, I was fed the lie that she did not know who I really was. In fact, I started to believe that she would despise the real me.

In that short time, Satan led me to believe that I was tainted and unworthy to be with someone so pure and innocent. Drastically, my emotions changed from feeling confident and at peace to feeling completely anxious, insecure, and shameful. I was in a full-on battle with the enemy, and it felt as if I were the one losing.

The intensity of these feelings took my full attention off of the moment, and I knew that the only way for it to end was to bring it into the light. So when we finally got to the hotel, I opened up to my wife about the war that was going on in my heart.

To my amazement, my beautiful bride showed me nothing but the grace and love of Christ. I can remember her patience as she lifted my shameful face and kissed me tenderly.

In my time of complete brokenness, my new bride provided strength, comfort, and affirmation. She laid her hands on me and prayed truth over me, reminding my heart and mind of who I really am in Christ: "Your past is not you; I *know* the real Greg…and I love him." And in this I experienced again the freedom found in Christ.

Although this spiritual battle felt like such a setback, I ended up learning some very valuable truths from it. One, my wife is breathtakingly amazing; and two, our enemy does not sit idle. He knows when we are the most vulnerable, and he will do anything in that moment to make us feel alone and shameful.

WHEN LUCIFER FELL

In the beginning, Satan was a lead angel for the heavenly army of God. In this role, he was named Lucifer, meaning "bringer of dawn" or "morning star." His job was to work closely with God while leading the rest of the angels in worshiping their Creator.

Although this sounds like a cool job to have, it soon became a huge source of jealousy. It is recorded in Isaiah that this "morning star" fell from heaven and was "thrust down into hell" because he desired to "ascend above the heights of the clouds" and become "like the Most High" (14:12-15).

In short, Lucifer, the bright light that he was, thought that he was and *should be* like God. Although he was beautiful, his prideful heart thought that he was more beautiful than the God who made him. Because of this, he started a conspiracy with other angels. He planted in them the same lie that he would later tell Adam and Eve: "You don't need God…He is holding out on us…we have the right to be like Him."

And slowly, one by one, he began gaining troops. His rebellion distorted his character and the character of every new follower. What they did not realize was that every lie that they believed turned them away from God and straight to Lucifer.

They went from one master to another; from worshiping the Lord to a want-to-be lord.

But this was his plan all along; to be served, praised, and adored by others. He wanted their worship. In his mind, oddly enough, he *deserved* their worship. And his corruption brought about their corruption. Although they were in a place that was full of love, they lost the ability to know that love.

So the inevitable happened—Lucifer and one third of the heavenly army were cast to hell. And as we know, God had no mercy on either him or his new followers.

THE ENEMY'S GOALS

Even though Satan was once called Lucifer, his new names will forever be the Adversary, the Evil One, the Father of Lies, and many more. Deep down, he has nothing but utter contempt for God and anything else that is good, especially His *new, holy,* and *righteous* children.

In fact, Satan is the absence of love and life, meaning that he can only hate and destroy. This is why he is said to be a devouring lion aiming to "steal, kill, and destroy" whatever possible (John 10:10). His obsession with himself led him to desire the worship and adoration that was only meant for God.

Soon this would lead him to convince God's beloved people to disobey and turn toward him as well (Genesis 3).

Although this is true, on a daily basis there are hundreds of humans who choose to turn back to their one true God. And above anything else, Lucifer *hates* for a "filthy, two legged" human to be restored by the *love* of the "Enemy."

In fact, every praise, shout, and chant for God that comes from the mouths of this "damned" creation makes him cringe. Therefore, his goal is simple: Keep his "children" away from that love and trick them into denying it daily.

You see, if he can get a believer to forget *who they are* through shaming them, then he can direct them away from being involved in those most hated praises, shouts, and chants. The more we deny God's love, the more we will stop intentionally worshiping Him. More than anything else, this pleases Satan, for his attack on us as believers is an attempt to *regain* our worship.

I have heard it said that Satan is both predictable and patient. He aims to tempt and lure us toward sin, deceive us from the truth, and accuse us with shame. Even though we can predict each of these tactics, we must not forget his obsessive patience. Without a doubt, he earnestly awaits for the right moment to act.

Temptations and Lures

The goal of temptations and lures has two main parts. The first is to get our eyes off of who we really are—a being now inseparable from our Creator—by acting outside of that calling (through sinning). And the second is to slowly construct a false self that is based solely from those actions.

The more we give into temptations and lures, the more we believe that we are what they are—sin. The actions of these temptations and lures can be anything, but the lie is always the same. We begin to believe that life, OUR life, will be better if we do them.

Lying, acts of rage, sexual immorality, lust, and greed—all of these are merely an outward display of a heart that has been tempted and lured toward believing that acting in such a way will *better it* as a whole. We sin because in the moment, we think it is the best way to go.

But every time we give into temptations and lures, we step deeper into the lie that there is a better way to live, one that is completely different than the full life that Jesus promises us. The end result, however, is never what we imagined it to be. We discover that nothing was truly fulfilled.

Although it promises much, sin leaves us feeling more desperate and broken than we ever did before.

This is when shame arises.

Deception

A dear professor of mine once said that Satan's main tactic is to deceive. If you think about it, here is a being who desires and longs for the worship of ALL of creation. This distorted passion falls apart when realizing that all of creation was made to worship their Creator *only*.

Therefore, the only way for him to be praised is to make the world believe that he is worthy of it. Deception is the only way for Satan to get his way, for it takes our eyes off of God and His truth and onto Satan and his lies.

Some of the typical acts of deception are aimed at getting us to focus on ourselves, making us see the world as ordinary, keeping us out of the present, and causing us to become blinded by a false reality.

A heart that is focused inwardly becomes selfish, bitter, and resentful. We become deceived in this way when we are consumed by the lie that our wants, needs, and concerns outweigh the rest of the world.

Think about it.

We fall into this deception when we are stuck in traffic, get a flat tire, in a line that is going super slow, or parenting a child who does not want to sleep. This lie leads us to believe that the day is owned by us individually. That's why we may get angry when it does not go our way.

My pastor once said, "We tend to believe that everyone who is going faster than us is a maniac, and everyone who is going slower than us is an idiot." And although you hate to admit it, this phrase may describe your own belief on an average day.

The second deception is centered on Satan luring us to believe that the world is ordinary. It is when our days become apathetic, typical, and mediocre that we forget the wonder and majesty of Christ.

I don't know about you, but my days can seem pretty "set."

I mean I wake up, shower, eat, drive the same car, take the same route, enter in the same doors at work, sit in the same chair at the same desk, and look with wide eyes at the same, long to-do list. And every week, I follow that same pattern.

I have heard it said that "too much familiarity can breed contempt" or—dare I say—*passivity*. To put it plainly, the more familiar something becomes, the less we take note of its extravagant details and the less aware we are toward its deeper meanings. If our days get too familiar and ordinary, then the miracle that *is* Christ is no longer seen or felt.

For God is intricately woven in the unseen; in the extraordinary.

The next deception, much like the previous ones, also takes our eyes off of Christ in our day. Satan's goal here is to cause us to focus on either the past or the future. Each of these pursuits distracts us from our present.

The enemy knows that it is in the present, *the now*, that God works. If we focus on the past, we choose to see things through a lens of the past, not letting us clearly see Jesus in the *now*. We become blind to His presence and the longing that He has to restore and transform us.

And if we consistently fear, look to, anticipate, or obsess about the future, we will not see the everyday tasks that God has for us now. Satan knows that it is through daily obedience that we become transformed into who we will be in the future.

Jamieson, Fausset, and Brown write this:

> "Tomorrow is the day when idle men work, and fools repent. Tomorrow is Satan's today; he cares not what good resolutions you form, if only you fix them for tomorrow."

Satan will constantly deceive us into putting off, until *tomorrow*, the actions and pursuits that we should be living out today. He knows, without a doubt, that "delayed obedience" is actually a powerful form of disobedience.

The last deception is built on Satan blinding us from reality. It encompasses all of the other deceptions and is the after-effect of temptations and lures. In fact, every deception is aimed at constructing this false reality.

Satan hopes to paint a new picture of life; one that is completely contrary to how it truly is and who we really are. And it is through this deception that he can tempt, lure, and deceive us even more.

Then come the accusations.

Accusations of Shame

Every temptation, lure, and deception allows Satan to sting us with more and more shame. They are as follows:

"You sinned and you failed."

"You will never be 'good' again."

"No one will love you after what you did."

"Your past will never be healed."

"No one will believe that you are actually going to change."

"You will never be who you want to become."

These accusations are a culmination of every temptation that we have given into and every deception that we have believed. It is the point where we believe our sin *is* us, so we keep doing it. And in a world consumed by our shameful selves, a world that is ordinary and plain, we find no redemption. Instead, we daily give into the lie that life is mediocre and we believe that our shameful life will never change; for nothing extraordinary can happen in an ordinary world, right?

So Satan accuses us more and more, while we sit idle and let him. The false reality that we have come to believe gives us no hope and no way out. Every accusation hits us deeply with regret. We continue to focus on our past sins and continue to feel the weight of each of them. And since we are already shameful, it becomes really hard to overcome their constant lures.

"You've already slipped once, so why not let it happen again?"

Yet deep down, we want our future to be different.

Satan knows this, so he gets us to focus on how it "should" be. But shame arises when we realize how different we are from how it "should" be. We are not as good, not as clean, not as productive, not as successful, and our family or marriage is nowhere close to being what we want it to be.

We become ashamed over and over again because we believe the lie that our life is not as extraordinary, righteous, or meaningful as it really is. But if Christ is truly one with us, then Satan has no ground in these accusations; for our failures, sins, and brokenness were all captured and overcome on the cross.

So in order for us to fight temptations, lures, deceptions, and every shameful accusation, and in order for us to see the reality of who we are and be changed by it, we must know and be consumed by *truth*. For truth is the foundation of change.

And it is through this that the shameless life can be discovered and lived out. So together, lets dive into some real truth.

QUESTIONS FOR REFLECTION

1. Have you ever experienced a moment of spiritual warfare? If so, write it out.

2. Look back at some of the common deceptions listed: *focusing on yourself, seeing the world as ordinary, staying out of the*

present, or being consumed by a false reality. Which one(s) of these are apparent in your life?

3. How has Satan used temptations, lures, and deception in your life to accuse you with shame?

PART 2

THE TRUTH

CHAPTER 5

THE WAY WE
ONCE WERE

In the image of God He created him;
male and female He created them...
The man and his wife were both
naked, and they felt no shame.
- Genesis 1:27; 2:25

Perfection is such a hard thing to grasp.

Much like beauty or taste, everyone's view of perfection is a little bit different. This broad term, in short, encompasses a state of being both complete and flawless.

To be perfect is to be without fault.

And if you think about it, each of us has our own opinion on what is both faulty and complete. But what amazes me is that both you and I—and the world as a whole—were originally created to be perfect. Unlike our wide range of definitions, however, this perfection was *one*.

At the beginning of time, humans were without blemish, given a world to rule and cultivate. Everything was *perfect*. Although this is true, an idea like this is so foreign to us. My view of what it meant to be perfect could be light-years away from someone else's view. And the funny thing is, we both are probably completely wrong.

Perfection, by no means, seems attainable or even understandable. But "perfect" once described humanity to the detail.

IT *WAS* GOOD

The Lord spoke creation into being.

His Spirit moved about, forming and shaping the world. Light beamed from the heavens and waves crashed around as the land exploded into existence. With beauty unimaginable, plants began to bud and grow, birds began to soar in the wind, and animals of all kinds made their home on the earth.

Within days, nothingness became beautiful and intricate.

Then, God *breathed* life into man, saw that he should not be alone, and formed from him a woman. Through understanding the depth of this perfect creation, we can uncover more about the tainting power of shame and then the rich identity that is restored to God's children.

> Then God said, "Let Us make man in Our image, according to Our likeness…" God created man in His own image, in the image of God He created him; male and female He created them.
>
> God blessed them; and God said to them, "Be fruitful and multiply, and fill the earth, and subdue it; and rule over the fish of the sea and over the birds of the sky and over every living thing that moves on the earth…." God saw all that He had made, and behold, it was very good.
>
> -Genesis 1:26-28; 31

When writing out this story, Moses must have really wanted his readers to understand two main things. First, we and all of creation were *created good*; and second, we, as humans, were *created* in God's *image*. These truths are said multiple times in the story of creation, highlighting their importance.

In fact, it is this "very good"-ness of creation that reveals true perfection. Once God had finished everything, He looked out and declared all of it *flawless, beautiful,* and *pleasing.* His masterpiece was complete, bringing Him joy and satisfaction.

The color, the scent, the warmth, and the majesty; everything that was made by His hands was perfect and created freely for His purpose.

And we, men and women, were created in His image. In God's perfect design of creation, He made humans *like* Him. This does not mean that we are physically like Him in our form and features, but we are like Him in the essence of our *soul.* Unlike any other created thing, humanity was given a soul that was in complete communion and unity with their Creator.

God made us like Him so that we could relate *to* Him.

Being in His likeness, Adam and Eve were able to know God in a way that other parts of creation could not.

The Purpose of Perfect People

Although all of creation was made complete in those first six days, this perfection still had a purpose. This is seen in the creation story with God "blessing" Adam and Eve. As image bearers of the Lord, they were given the task of naming, cultivating, subduing, and ruling over the rest of creation.

Yes, the world was *complete*, but God desired for men and women to work amidst the completeness. To be honest, this is hard for me to fully grasp. Even though all of creation was perfect and finished, there were still things that needed to be done, things that were commanded to be done. And being made in God's likeness, both Adam and Eve were the ones for the job.

Although perfect, the world still had potential. And although complete, humanity still had the purpose of bringing out that potential.

Just as God *spoke* creation into existence, Adam was able to *speak* or appoint a name for every other created thing. This shows that God desired His image bearers to have "creative ownership" over the land. In fact, His exact words are that they "subdue" and "rule" over the rest of creation.

This touches on mankind's dominion over all other nature. Because their souls were like God, they were created to be conquerors over everything else in the world. All of creation was under them because they were God's representatives; His heirs.

Although this is true, their kingship enabled them to not just rule over the world, but to also take care of it. In its beautiful state, the world still needed to be cared for. It needed to be cultivated. And it was humanity's mission to sustain and bring about life all across the world. This was the blessing given to them, one that they would do alongside of their Creator.

Although God and man were not equals, there is a beautiful partnership in this blessing. As they went along, their work proclaimed and mirrored the creative work of God. With every action, their Lord was given glory and honor. Their power was His power, their rule was His rule, and their work was His work.

As they moved along the earth, He moved with them.

The Heart, Mind, and Soul of Perfect People

Like a beautiful aroma enveloping all aspects of a room, perfection touched much deeper than we tend to think. In fact, goodness and completeness were found in the essence of Adam and Eve.

And above our ability to even comprehend was the perfection and clarity that each had in their heart, mind, and soul. Where we have confusion and chaos, they had unity and peace. Their perception of the world, themselves, and their Creator was complete; not lacking anything.

There was no forgetfulness, no blind spots, no walled-up hearts, and absolutely no distrust. Their physical state of being naked and uncovered mirrored the innocent and open state of their hearts. In this complete openness, Adam and Eve knew only one thing: God.

> For by Him all things were created: things in heaven
> and on earth, visible and invisible, whether thrones or
> powers or rulers or authorities; all things were created
> by Him and for Him. He is before all things, and in
> Him all things hold together.
>
> -Colossians 1:16-17

Normally when this verse is read, it is read through the context of our time now, after the fall of man. Even though this is a great way to read it, I think it shows just how perfect we once were.

In Him all things were created.

And in Him all things hold together.

I do not know about you, but these concepts blow my mind. I would even say that our small minds cannot even come close to grasping what they really mean.

You see, in our God, all things came about. Now this is not just those things that are visible to us; like you, me, your dog, the stars, the planets, and the sun. No, this is more than that. Paul says that even the *invisible* things were created by God.

Yes, the invisible things. All around us is a world that our eyes cannot see. A world that is spiritual; a world that is constantly at war; and a world that is grander than anything we can dream up. And *by God*, THAT was created.

But Paul does not stop here. He also says that *everything*, both visible and invisible, is constantly held together by our God. He is in, through, and even encompasses all things. It is because of Him that we are even held together.

Mind blowing, I know. But this means that our everyday life is missing the realization of these truths:

Why can we not see God literally holding all things together?

Why can we not actually see Him in all things?

If in reality, our God is ever present, meaning He is always there and is holding all things together, then we must be missing such a large chunk of true reality. What is even more unbelievable is that all of this was once known by humanity; known in a way that was perfect, complete, and absolute. With every glance, Adam and Eve saw God.

Just as I said before, their minds only comprehended one thing: their Lord. And it was by that one thing that they could comprehend everything, both visible and invisible. God made all things make sense to them.

Because they could clearly see and know that God was in all things and held all things together, their everyday sights displayed Him vividly. When they saw a flower bud, a bird soar, and even the sun rise, they saw...they *saw* God. They literally saw Him living and moving.

In perfection, there was no disunion between things. Adam and Eve had knowledge of the connection between all of creation; they saw God's fingerprints, His DNA on everything around them; including themselves.

You see, they not only saw God living in, moving in, and holding together everything around them, but they also knew that He was living in, moving in, and holding *them* together.

Their *only* view of self was through the view, the lens, of God.

This is huge. They did not doubt themselves, they did not see themselves as "less than," and they did not define themselves as being naked and shameful.

They saw and understood reality. God not only held them together, but unlike all other creation, they were in His image. They were valued, loved, and cared for.

> In the image of God He created him; male and female
> He created them…And the man and his wife were
> both naked, and they felt no shame.
>
> -Genesis 1:27; 2:25

When perfection ruled the world, nakedness was the norm. In fact, humanity was once a beautiful culmination of being *very* good, naked, and unashamed of it all.

In the midst of perfection, Adam and Eve were exposed and it did not affect them. This is because "exposure" is a term that was not even understood by them; they had no concept of nakedness and no need to be clothed. A life like this would be so amazing.

And it was through being genuine and unbound that they could see God around them and in them. It was not in their nature to cover up or make defenses. In fact, each of these pursuits would distract them from their blessed purpose.

They were complete, and completeness does not need additional clothing. In God's likeness, they were who they were made to be and were proud of it. They openly and genuinely ruled as heirs to God's Kingdom, cultivating it as commanded.

In Eden, they were not troubled with the fears of being *naked* and unbound by the shame that accompanied it. But oh, how far we have come from this definition and experience of perfection.

QUESTIONS FOR REFLECTION

1. What is your view of perfection?

2. Why do you think God created the perfect world to still have potential? What docs that say about us?

3. Search the Bible to see what the Word says about perfection.

4. How often do you view the world through God's lens? What would it look like to see yourself and others like this?

Chapter 6

When Perfection Became Ashamed

Then the eyes of both of them were opened,
and they knew that they were naked.
- Genesis 3:7

"In the knowledge of good and evil, man knows his own
possibilities; his possibility of being good and evil."
- D. Bonhoeffer

Your eyes open and you are being rushed through a narrow hallway. Your thoughts are going crazy as you search left and right for some kind of familiarity, but nothing catches your eyes.

"What…what am I doing?"

"Where am I?"

"How did I get here?"

Holding tightly to both of your arms are the hands of two people whom you have never met before. Together, they are eagerly pulling you ahead toward the door found at the end of the hallway.

As you hurry along, you pass by large men in suits. You notice that they each nod at you as you pass by. It is as though they are silently cheering you on for what is ahead.

"What is ahead?"

You reach the door and another suited man opens it. At once your two escorts pat you on the back and gently push you through. As they close the door behind you, everything turns black. You take a few steps forward, and at once the lights flash on.

You are in a large auditorium.

It does not take long for you to realize that the lights are only on you. Millions of people are clapping, waiting for what you are going to say. Nerves shoot through your veins and you decide to take your eyes away from all of the faces in front of you.

And instantly your heart drops.

Either you are wearing a fantastic, skin-colored onesie or you are stark naked. You look out into the auditorium to see laughing and taunting faces, all pointing directly at your horrific display of public nudity.

You scream while earnestly seeking something to hide behind. In the midst of your panic, you awaken and find yourself at home in your bed, sweating and shaking.

Maybe you have not experienced a dream exactly like this, but the truth is that many of us have had this kind of "naked nightmare" at least once or twice in our lifetime.

But what is it about this dream that binds us with fear and fills us with shame? I personally think that it has a lot to do with our fear of being inexplicably *exposed*. Ingrained in us is a knowledge that tells us that true exposure is bad.

Deep down, we often think: "If people see me as I see me…the exposed, naked, and messed up me…then they will, without a doubt, point and mock."

In this world, genuine honesty, vulnerability, openness, and exposure are not *natural*. They seem like ideas from an alternate reality, scenes from those sappy TV shows, or aspects of a fairy tale.

But these are characteristics found in the world that God created for us to live in. And as we know by now, perfection allowed Adam and Eve to be naked and unashamed of it.

They could each proudly stand up straight, representing their fantastic, skin-colored onesies, without any hesitation at all.

THEN IT CAME

Although once perfect, something drastically happened to the world. Without skipping a beat, the record of the "fall of man" is written back-to-back from the record of God's perfect creation. It is literally *right* after the sentence of humanity being unashamed.

And in his attempt to destroy God's beautiful design, Satan comes into the scene in the form of a snake—a *talking* snake:

> Now the serpent was more crafty than any other wild animal that the LORD God had made. He said to the woman….
>
> -Genesis 3:1

Instantly we see Satan slithering up to have a chat with Eve.

Surprisingly, she gives him her full attention, as if a talking animal were an everyday occurrence. But it is in this little conversation that Satan imposes uncertainty in her heart. In the form of questions, Satan slowly deceives Eve into doubting God and His commands while tempting her toward disobedience:

> Did God say, "You shall not eat from any tree in the garden?" The woman said to the serpent, "We may eat of the fruit of the trees in the garden; but God said,

'You shall not eat of the fruit of the tree that is in the middle of the garden, nor shall you touch it, or you shall die.'" But the serpent said to the woman, "You will not die; for God knows that when you eat of it your eyes will be opened, and you will be like God, knowing good and evil."

-Genesis 3:1-5

Eve answers Satan's question, but it was her inner curiosity and doubt that he wanted to stir up. In this curiosity, Eve is slowly tricked into questioning things. I can picture the wheels turning in her head: *"Is that really what God said? Why would He keep this tree from us? What is so bad about it?"*

The craftiness of the serpent got both her and Adam to wonder if God was keeping something from them; if there was a "hidden knowledge" that He wanted to deny them. And as these doubts grew, Adam and Eve acted.

They wanted to uncover the "secret" and discover the knowledge that would *truly* make them like God, as if they were not close enough to Him already. So they took the fruit and bit into this source of *knowledge*. They bought into the lies of Satan and dramatically disobeyed their Creator.

Then the eyes of both of them were opened, and they knew that they were naked; and they sewed fig leaves together and made themselves loin coverings.

-Genesis 3:7

In one instance, their eyes became opened and they gained the knowledge of being *naked*. Now, when first reading this, it does seem to insinuate that both Adam and Eve were "blind" or had some kind of hindrance beforehand.

But the comprehension and insight *gained* by this act made their created perfection, beauty, and purpose become *lost*.

If you think back, before the fall, man only knew one thing: God.

When created, they were given the knowledge of reality, and through God, they could see all things clearly. But due to their disobedience, this knowledge was altered and dramatically lessened, making them see things differently than ever before.

The knowledge they now obtained twisted their view of themselves and of the world around them. It is not the kind of knowledge one would gain through taking a class or reading a book. This knowledge signified the complete reversal of what man once knew, tainting them with fears and insecurities.

Dietrich Bonhoeffer, a well-known theologian and pastor, wrote about this drastic change:

> "In the knowledge of good and evil, man does not understand himself in the reality of the destiny that was appointed to him, but rather he knows his own possibilities; his possibility of being good and evil."

Instead of Adam and Eve knowing themselves in and through God, they now saw themselves outside of Him. Even though this seems like a small change, its repercussions are not. You see, their perception was once complete, but now it became limited and lost.

The knowledge of good and evil is a knowledge that was not designed for mankind. And now that they possessed it, their view of everything was seen only through themselves. In this perception, they both saw and felt the wretched creatures they had become.

Their open eyes also allowed them to clearly see all of the disunity made through their sin. Unlike ever before, they recognized that they were outside of God; and *nothing* outside of God is good.

Through their act of disobedience, man became *fallen*.

In an instance, they saw how needy and incomplete they were apart from their Lord. Because they had lost all bonds with each other and with God, openness and vulnerability did not seem ideal. So without hesitation, they built up barriers and sought protection through clothing. In their new knowledge, they were no longer complete.

The secret that they hoped to uncover through this fruit was a secret that they could not handle, one that would bring about humanity's downfall. And here, the concept of nakedness was born, and with it, *shame*. Bonhoeffer writes:

> "Man covers himself, conceals himself from men and from God. Covering is necessary because it keeps shame awake, and with it the memory of the disunion with God and also man.... He must now withdraw himself and must live in concealment."

Perfection and shame have no place together. They are in opposition. Perfection glorifies God while shame glorifies sin. And because of Adam and Eve's disobedience, God could no longer be one with them.

This is because in their sin, they became sin.

God's goodness cannot be present in any way with sin. So against His wishes, He sent them out of the garden. This was their punishment. His precious creation not only became separated from Him spiritually, but now physically as well.

This original sin that they committed did not just hurt them. It also had a ripple effect on all of creation. Heaven and earth were separated and the entire world, the kingdom they were blessed to rule over, was cursed along with them.

Darkness now took the place of light and the ground became hardened, swarming with thorns and thistles. Adam and Eve saw visibly the incredible disunity and chaos that they caused. The world and everything in it was no longer perfect, and it was all because of them. They were deeply ashamed.

The saddest part of all is that this shame was valid.

Once man and woman sinned, they became *sinful*. God was no longer their perception; their center. Without a doubt, humanity deserved the shame of this sin.

And Satan, the enemy, was pleased by all of it.

Fallen and Shameful

Although he was cursed for what he did, the serpent seems to win a large battle here. With goodness being no more, evil was able to abound. Now that God was "out of the picture," Satan could roam around and rule the whole of it.

The fallen earth, and everything in it, became under his reign. Although this is true, it does not mean that God was not in control. Because of sin's presence in the world, He allowed and still allows Satan to rule and exercise authority.

But Satan has no power over God.

Fallen man, however, is another story.

As the "god of this world," Satan was able to reign over humanity's corrupted state. Because Adam and Eve became sinful and shameful, they fell under the power and lure of his words. He could now slither around and work among humanity.

And all around them was the constant reminder of the curse that they had provoked. What once was became only a memory, as they fell further into despair. Apart from God, their hearts became wicked, their pursuits became rebellious, and their minds became drenched with Satan's lies.

> The earth is defiled by its people; they have disobeyed the laws, violated the statutes and broken the everlasting covenant. Therefore a curse consumes the earth; its people must bear their guilt.
>
> - Isaiah 24:5-6a

In the enemy's mind, God's "image bearers" were now *his*. Because of their broken covenant, Satan now had control over every one of their thoughts and actions. The lies he led them to believe and the actions he persuaded them to commit enabled him to constantly throw the nature of their fallen state back in God's face: *"Just remember...YOU created these failures."*

And his reign over fallen humanity continues today.

But God wasn't, isn't, and has never been done with mankind; He *knows* us and loves us. Because of this, God sought to do whatever possible to have a relationship with us again. And as we know, He would soon send His perfection to become shame, in order for shame to once again become His perfection.

But if you can remember from Chapter 4, the ruler of this earth had and continues to have a game plan. Through humanity's shame, Satan would blind them. Through humanity's shame, he would use them. And through humanity's shame, he would do whatever possible to control them.

QUESTIONS FOR REFLECTION

1. In the perfect world, Adam and Eve fell because they felt as if God was holding something back from them. Do you feel like this at times? If so, when?

2. Where you are now, do you feel that you have to build up walls in order to protect yourself? If so, why?

3. Look back at the two quotes from Dietrich Bonhoeffer. How do they relate to each other and how are they seen in your life?

Chapter 7

The Shame Bearer

For our sake He made Him to be sin who
knew no sin, so that in Him we might
become the righteousness of God.
-2 Corinthians 5:21

There is a stark contrast between darkness and light.

It is something that we all know very well.

It is in the instant flash of a camera, the short glare of sunlight on a cloudy day, the illuminated phone in the pitch-black movie theater, the blinding fridge light when all you want is a midnight snack, and in the oh-so-hated morning sunlight that breaks through your window.

What I find funny is that all of these moments, even though we know they are coming, still seem to catch us off guard. They happen and our eyes frantically try to catch up with the change.

The effects of these lights are literally blinding. And our initial response is always the same. We halfway close our eyes, turn our face away, or use a hand, pillow, or other object to make our own source of shade. In every case, the light is so shocking, so blinding, because we have become so used to the darkness.

Think about it.

In darkness, our eyes become accustomed to seeing nothing. If there is a little light, they may work well enough for us to make out objects and dodge walls. But in complete blackness, there is simply nothing to be seen. Our eyes become dull and unaware of anything except the darkness.

And in that state, they settle.

Darkness becomes the norm.

And this is very similar to the world that Adam and Eve had become accustomed to. Their rebellion "turned the lights out" and left them full of shame in a cursed world. Darkness became the new norm and slowly the eyes of their hearts became accustomed to it.

Although the Lord consistently tried to light up their path, His beloved creation continued to shade themselves from it. So He sent them a promise: that His *light* would soon come into the world with the hope that all would see it and be brought out of darkness.

And it was into this dark world that Jesus came.

Regardless of your familiarity with this story, I challenge you to read on and gain new insight into Jesus' connection with shame.

A MESSAGE OF LIGHT AND LIFE

> In him was life, and the life was the light of men. The light shines in the darkness, and the darkness has not overcome it…The true light, which gives light to everyone, was coming into the world…yet the world did not know him.
>
> -John 1:4-5; 9-10

When Jesus entered the world, He, being light and life, came into a place that was full of darkness and death. Jesus, being fully God, was a clear picture of perfection. His desire was to bring life and righteousness to all men, granting their hearts and their souls a way out of the darkness.

Like a bright flash in the night, many people shielded their eyes from the truth that He brought. The only life that they had known was one of sin, pain, and selfishness. This was their norm and the eyes of their hearts were in no way ready to adjust to His brightness.

In fact, John says that the world *did not recognize Him* (1:10). Their blindness and numbness made them miss the life that Jesus was bringing. They knew that something was different about Him, but they saw this difference as something to shade their hearts from.

> Yet to all who received Him, to those who believed
> in His name, He gave the right to become children
> of God—children born not of natural descent, nor of
> human decision or a husband's will, but born of God.
>   -John 1:12-13

To those who did believe, they were given an opportunity to have a complete life change. Like the contrast between darkness and light, through Him they were *given the right* to become children of God. The eyes of their hearts took that blinding leap of faith and became consumed with the warmth of His light.

They began following Him, calling themselves His disciples. This now became the new norm for them, a life that was defined by eternal life. Apart from this Light, they were nothing, but receiving Him allowed them to be born of God. Being with Jesus, these disciples became "children of light." Through their faith, night became day.

The whole gospel of John speaks of Jesus' ministry as one that continually proclaims life and light. Jesus repeatedly told His followers of His Father sending Him to bring about a Kingdom of Light. And at the end of His life, Jesus warned His disciples that the day would soon turn into darkness again (12:35).

Although this seems confusing, He was merely predicting His own death. He spoke that an hour would come where the darkness would seem to be overbearing. And on the day of Jesus' death, at high noon, the daylight turned to darkness. It was a visual picture of what was going on spiritually. Jesus, the Light of the world, had just died. But only through this would mankind be able to live.

The reason is this: Even though His disciples were given the right to become children of God, at their core, they were still in darkness. They experienced light only because *He* was in their presence, but that Light had not yet become one with them. This is why darkness came back when Jesus died; the light left the world.

In order for His light to become one with humanity, their punishment, our punishment, had to be paid for. As you know by now, in our fallen nature, God cannot be one with us. And because God cannot be one with us, we deserve separation and punishment.

Although Jesus' light was changing His disciples, the core of who they were had to be changed as well. This would be done through a God-man dying in the place of each and every one of them. Darkness had to overcome Jesus so that His light would overcome humanity's darkness.

Jesus said it Himself, "Put your trust in the Light while you have it, so that you may become sons of Light" (John 12:36).

THE ONE WHO BORE

On this earth, Jesus chose to bear our shame.

Let me say that again: on this earth, Jesus chose to bear, take on, and become *our* shame. We read over and over in scripture that He took our darkness and our sins to the cross, but I believe that we overlook that He also *bore our shame.*

For darkness is one with shame and its only purpose is to isolate, blind, and destroy. If Jesus took on our sins, He also took on the shame that accompanies each and every one of them. He bore the *whole* world's shame.

Just hours before Jesus' trial, He is found journeying to pray in the garden of Gethsemane. He took His faithful disciples with Him. Before praying in the darkness of night, Jesus told His dear followers that He was suffering: "My soul is overwhelmed with sorrow to the point of death" (Mark 14:34).

I cannot imagine the pain found in His eyes as He disclosed what was going on inside of Him. Honestly I do not think that words could adequately describe even an ounce of what He was going through. His soul, the deepest part of His being, was overwhelmed and distressed with sorrow.

But up until this moment, He kept these feelings to Himself.

Have you ever wondered what was going through Jesus' mind those few short hours before His betrayal? What led Him to feel so overwhelmed with sorrow?

The Journey to Gethsemane

As the group quietly walked out of the city and toward Gethsemane, I can only wonder what images were coming to Jesus' mind. The very word "Gethsemane" means *olive press*, perhaps speaking to the weight of suffering that Jesus would endure both there and the next day while on the cross.

Like olives being crushed in order to harvest the oil, Jesus would be crushed in an intense press of grief and sadness.

Being who He was, Jesus knew in detail what was coming up. Judas had just left to betray Him and now His Father's plans were in motion. He knew what was next. And every step toward Gethsemane was one step closer to that pressing place, ultimately leading Him to His death.

Without a doubt, He foresaw the taunting voices, the painful beatings, the scornful crown, the shameful spit, and the sinner's cross that were all awaiting Him. Each of these acts would place our deserved shame and darkness upon Him. And in the darkness and silence of the night, Jesus somberly walked on, His heart pounding and His soul already deeply grieving.

He understood that the silence and stillness of the night would have to come to an end. Soon, the mocking voices of His very own people would be the only thing to hear.

As we know, the Jews, God's chosen people, shaded their eyes from the light that Christ brought and chose to dispose of Him. They denied that He was the Messiah and accused Him of wrongs that He had no part of.

He was called a blasphemer and a slanderer. These titles were given to degrade someone, labeling them wretched and evil. They called him *evil*. The Jews wrongly labeled Jesus as a disgrace. Although the officials saw no wrong in Him, the Jews persistently shouted that He was guilty and therefore deserved death.

So even though He was walking with His friends, I am sure that He already felt the sting of betrayal. Instead of the adoration and praise that He deserved, He would soon encounter curses and scorn. Perfection should never have been accused of being evil. And perfection certainly did not deserve punishment.

Although the words would sting, Jesus knew that they would also be accompanied by physical attacks. He would be struck, flogged, beaten, and mutilated. He knew that the face and body that His disciples now saw would soon become unrecognizable.

It did not matter that they had been with Him for years; He understood that what was to come would destroy His body, His image. The soft, warm smile, the tender touch, and the humble posture that He had carried all of His life would soon vanish through multiple beatings.

In a matter of hours, Jesus would become ugly, disgusting, and deformed. The image forced upon Him would be one to turn your eyes from; parents would deliberately keep this sight from the eyes of their innocent children.

Soon, His own Kingdom would no longer recognize Him.

But a King He was. And it was the unwavering confidence in this truth that kept Him from falling in to Satan's temptations. But as He walked to the garden, Jesus understood that His kingship would soon be mocked. Humans, the very people that He was sent to rescue, would deny His crown of gold and give Him a crown of thorns.

Thorns were not meant to touch perfection.

In fact, it was man's sin that led God to curse the ground with thorns. They were a picture of disobedience, corruption, and shame. Being the product of fallen man, their only purpose is to entangle, overwhelm, and bring death to every ounce of life around them. Although this is true, Jesus knew that in spite of Him, the soldiers would twist together these objects of sin and force them upon His head.

If that was not enough, the sweat from His brows would also be accompanied with the saliva of each one of His torturers. In just a few short hours, the King of Kings would wear a sinner's crown and the spit that came with it.

His heart knew of the weight of all this. He even knew that upon His shoulders would soon be a guilty man's cross and upon His shoulders would soon be the weight of the world's sin.

Every bit of suffering would culminate and peak in that moment; the accusations, the lies, the beatings, the thorns, and the spit. And looking forward with a heavy heart, Jesus knew that He would gladly take on all of it.

Every bit of shame would soon be His.

A Prayer Like No Other

When reaching Gethsemane, every thought and image led Jesus to finally disclose the intensity of His feelings. More than anything, He wanted to be close to people who still loved Him.

"Remain here and keep watch with Me," He told them.

And after walking a few steps from His friends, scripture says that He fell on His face to pray. His whole life had led Him to what was about to happen and He was overwhelmed with the pressure and sadness of it all.

With a humble and submissive heart, Jesus began praying: "Father, if you are willing, remove this cup from me. Nevertheless, not my will, but yours, be done" (Luke 22:42).

Jesus saw everything that He would have to endure; all of the pain and shame, and in His humanity, He longed for there to be another way. Although He would do whatever His Father commanded of Him, He still desired something different.

This, in itself, shows just how terrible of a responsibility it was to carry, wear, and become man's sin. Jesus, perfect in every way, knew that this cup would be incredibly hard to drink. With the weight pressing down on Him, His inner pain was soon seen outwardly.

> And being in agony he prayed more earnestly; and his
> sweat became like great drops of blood falling down
> to the ground.
>
> -Luke 22:44

Like an olive press separating the oil from the plant, the weight of this prayer literally caused Jesus to sweat blood. The suffering that He was going through was because of the shame that He would soon become. The King of Kings bled from His pores in anticipation of what He would soon do for those He loved.

Don't Miss This

In the blackness of night, Jesus prayed to His Father. In hindsight, we know that regardless of His pain, He still chose to go through with everything. And after ending His prayer, He headed back to His followers.

To His amazement, they were sleeping.

It was the very eve of His death, and His friends were snoozing. Although they could not understand the depth of Jesus' sorrow, it seems they should have known not to fall asleep. He needed them. But one by one, they each fell into slumber.

They allowed their heavy eyes to shut out what was truly happening in that garden. More than anything else, this shows that they did not get it. They did not understand that their leader, the man who brought them through so many things, would soon become *their* sin, *their* shame, and *their* disobedience.

Although I would love to end this chapter right now, my conviction is that we still miss this incredible truth today.

We know that Jesus hung on a cross and died for us. But please do not discount the fact that the only reason He bled was because He became *our* sin and *our* shame. And the only reason that He became *our* sin and *our* shame was so He could make us perfect again; to bring us back into completeness and into His light.

On that cross, He became shame. And three days later, He defeated it; He became victorious. He made a way for shameful humans to be perfected once again. For all of our shame was nailed to the cross.

Righteous Jesus became shame so that shameful humans could become His righteousness; His perfection.

Don't allow the eyes of your heart to shut out the truth of what happened on that cross. It is what allows us to connect with Christ, to confidently approach his throne, and to experience healthy shame in the light of His greatness.

And as we will soon uncover in the next chapter, Jesus' work on the cross is what gives us the opportunity to live an unashamed and victorious life now.

QUESTIONS FOR REFLECTION

1. Recall a time – maybe it is even now – where darkness was/is your "norm." What were/are the reasons for this?

2. What thoughts and feelings swarm in your mind when you read that Jesus chose to bear *your* shame?

3. How have you allowed the eyes of your heart to shut out this truth in the past?

CHAPTER 8

WE NOW STAND UNASHAMED

"Outside of Christ, I am only a sinner, but in Christ, I am saved. Outside of Christ, I am empty; in Christ, I am full. Outside of Christ, I am weak; in Christ, I am strong. Outside of Christ, I have been defeated; in Christ, I am already victorious. How meaningful are the words, 'in Christ...'"
- Watchman Nee

I love that there are multiple sides to a story.

No matter how simple one may be, it never fails to find a different perspective; a different version of the same tale. We see this best portrayed in the lives of children:

> *"Dad...Jack hit me."*
> *"No I didn't, she pushed me down first!"*
> *"Nu-huhhh!"*

And the stories begin.

Yes, it may be true that one was hit and the other was pushed down, but as we all know, there is more to this story. They each had something to do with it.

In fact, it would be both unfair and bad parenting to choose to take one version of the story over the other. And I am confident that the majority of you know this. It seems like common sense to hear all sides before moving on with a response.

It is not that one is better than the other or more true, but it is through hearing every version or perspective that a fuller picture of the story can be found. When we see all sides, the story grows in depth and takes on much more meaning.

We discover that the problem started long before the push was made; that each of their hurt feelings led to their actions. It is after seeing every perspective that the *true real truth* can be found.

HE AND WE ARE ONE

I say all of this to reveal the beauty of the Gospels. Last chapter, we left off with Jesus in the Garden of Gethsemane. A major aspect of this evening was the conversation that Jesus had with His Father. But what John records in his gospel is another version of this prayer.

Being one of the three that were positioned closest to Jesus while praying, I can imagine John eagerly listening in on what his Lord was saying. And in John's version of this prayer, Jesus not only prays for Himself, but also for both His twelve followers and the millions of those that will follow in the future.

You see, in Jesus' prayer, just hours before His death, He prays for us—for both you and me:

> I pray also for those who will believe in Me through
> their message, that all of them may be one. Father,
> just as You are in Me and I am in You. May they also
> be in Us so that the world may believe that You have

sent Me. I have given them the glory that You gave
Me, that they may be one as We are one: I in them
and You in Me....

-John 17:20-23

After Jesus accepts that His Father's will was for Him to continue
on toward death, He turns His focus on those that love Him. Even
though He is about to take on all of our sin, shame, and punishment,
He still chooses to pray for us. And what He says is key.

First, He wants us to be one with each other so that His kingdom
can be united. But secondly, He lets us in on the fact that we are
already one with Him.

I find it completely beautiful that He transitions into praying for
those of us living today. After focusing on all of the weight of sin and
shame that would soon be His, Jesus chooses to look toward the effect
that it will have on us. In that moment, He looked forward to giving
us His glory, becoming one with us, and ultimately having His whole
Kingdom united.

The very reason that we can be one with each other is because He
has allowed us to be one with Him.

The glory given to us is *His* glory. And this is found in the Holy
Spirit within us. Being followers of Jesus allows us to become one with
Him; all separation has been taken away and His Spirit now dwells
forever in us.

We were therefore buried with Him through baptism
into death in order that, just as Christ was raised from
the dead through the glory of the Father, we too may
live a new life.

If we have been united with Him like this in His
death, we will certainly also be united with Him in
His resurrection...anyone who has died has been
freed from sin.

-Romans 6:4-5, 7

He died so that our sin would die. And His defeat over death and
His resurrection from the grave allowed us to be free from sin. The
life that we have is one that is new and united to Him.

When Christ was on that cross, He was there for you and me.
And Paul writes in Colossians that the cross "disarmed the power
and authorities" of the world and that Jesus "made a public spectacle
of them by triumphing over them" (2:15). He is stating that Jesus'
victory over death literally *mocked* every power and authority that
stood against Him.

Jesus' triumph *mocked* Satan.

Paul continues with saying that our lives are now forever hidden
in Jesus; forever hidden in that glory and power.

Perfection is Restored

In this new life, aspects of perfection are once more.

Yes, you read that correctly.

Through the blood of Jesus and His defeat of sin, we, as followers
of Him, are perfected in Him. Because He is perfect, our lives, our
souls, and our destiny are now perfect.

You are no longer sinful; *you are complete; perfect.*

But this is hard for you to believe.

Even now, you are feeling an uncertainty about that sentence.
Deep down, you feel as if it is a lie. You certainly do not feel perfect. I
know all of this because it is just as hard for me to write it down as it

is for you to read. But the truth is that through Christ, I am perfect; I am righteous; and I am His.

Once again, however, I must draw your attention away from the number of definitions that come to your mind when you hear the word perfect. Many times, the very reason we deny the label of being "perfect" is because we have a false idea of what that really means. The truth is, every definition that you have is man-made. But the perfection that we have in Christ is God-made.

Being new and united with Him, we are once again found in Him. Our life was once consumed by darkness, but in an instant, night turned to day, bringing us into a new reality—a true reality.

We now have the opportunity, through the Holy Spirit, to once again see all things through God. Our life, and therefore perception, is no longer apart from Him.

Just like Adam and Eve in the Garden, we now have the opportunity to see things through Him again; for salvation restores the effects of sin. Blindness becomes enlightened. Brokenness becomes healed. Separation becomes united. And shame becomes righteousness and perfection.

In His prayer, Jesus implies that we can be one with each other only because He has made us one with Him. If we were still shameful and sinful, this would not be so.

For the effects of sin and shame do nothing but destroy, separate, and taint. If we are one with Christ and are called to be one with each other, then we must already be freed from the effects of sin and shame.

He changed us. Our lives, regardless of how distant we feel or how terrible our desires may be, are perfect in Christ. And unlike before, this perfection can never again be lost.

Although we still mess up and choose to disobey God, our life is forever out of sin's hold. The apostle Paul writes that sin is no longer our master; that even though we give into it, it can never again define us (Galatians 4 & 5).

Because we are one with Christ, we are also one with His victory over sin. And God in us, the Holy Spirit, allows us to conquer sin. If you can remember, when God created man, He called them to rule with Him. And through Jesus, our perfect state has been restored, allowing us to once again be rulers.

> Who shall separate us from the love of Christ? Shall trouble or hardship or persecution or famine or nakedness or danger or sword?...No, in all these things we are more than conquerors through Him who loved us. For I am convinced that neither death nor life, neither angels nor demons, neither the present nor future, nor any powers, neither height nor depth, nor anything else in all creation, will be able to separate us from the love of God that is in Christ Jesus our Lord.
>
> -Romans 8:35-39

This is the truth found in Christ. In Him, bondage is no more. We are rulers and nothing can separate us from that. I love that Paul includes "nakedness" within this list. Although each of these problems have the potential to bring about shame in our life, scripture clearly and countlessly teams up nakedness with its effect of shame.

Yet if we are conquerors over nakedness, then this, once again, reveals that shame no longer has power over us. Much like Adam and Eve in perfection, we can be exposed, open, vulnerable, and genuine without feeling shame. It is God's love that makes us unashamed.

Now, I am not suggesting that you leave your clothes behind and become an avid nudist. What I am suggesting is that your need to conceal sins, hide your fears, and withdraw when anxious is something that you no longer have to experience. There is no shame in Christ.

As Paul says, nothing in creation, *absolutely nothing* can separate us from that love. As conquerors, we are heirs to God's Kingdom. We are born into an inheritance "that can never perish, spoil or fade" (1 Peter 1:4). And in this inheritance, we are forever "shielded" by God's great power (1:5).

SERVANTS OF RIGHTEOUSNESS

I do not know if you have ever read the book of Isaiah, but it is one of my favorite books of the Old Testament. He, like many prophets in his day, was a bold proclaimer of truth.

One of the most well-known sections of Isaiah is the one that tells of "The Servant of the Lord." Starting in Chapter 47, Isaiah begins to prophesy, or foretell, of a coming Savior that would appear and be the Messiah to all.

He is said to be a light to those perishing; One that will bring salvation to the ends of the earth. Although we know of Him as Jesus, Isaiah chooses to only use the word "Servant" to describe Him.

Unlike the world, this Servant is completely obedient:

See, My Servant will act wisely; He will be raised and lifted up and highly exalted. Just as there were many who were appalled at Him—His appearance was so disfigured beyond that of any man…He was led like a lamb to the slaughter…My righteous Servant will justify many and He will bear their iniquities.

-Isaiah 52:13-14; 53:7-11

Before Jesus ever came to earth, Isaiah beautifully wrote of the work that He would do for us. Like a lamb to the slaughter, He would die so that He could justify many and make them like Him.

And Isaiah continues. But as he writes, his attention begins to shift from the Servant's work to the effects that it will have on all of humanity. He writes of what Jesus' death means for us. Please let these words of truth sink deep into your hearts.

Isaiah is speaking to all of us:

> Do not be afraid; you will not suffer shame. Do not fear disgrace; you will not be humiliated. You will forget the shame of your youth and remember no more the reproach of your widowhood. For your Maker is your husband—the Lord Almighty is His name—the Holy One of Israel is your Redeemer; He is called the God of all the earth.

-Isaiah 54:4-5

Because of what the *Servant of the Lord* did for you and me, we will never again suffer shame. In fact, when Isaiah writes that first sentence, he uses the same Hebrew phrase as Moses did in Genesis. Just as Adam and Eve were naked and unashamed, we will stand unashamed.

No matter who we once were or the label that the world tries to put on us, we will forever be righteous because of our Redeemer. In fact, Peter writes that God's divine power has granted us all things that pertain to *life*. And through His promises we "participate in that divine nature, having escaped the corruption in the world caused by evil desires" (2 Peter 1:4). Because of Jesus, we can participate in God's divine nature; for we are righteous.

The Shame of Our Youth

And there is more to find in Isaiah. He writes *"You will forget the shame of your youth...."*

Because it is an Old Testament writing, we must remember that Isaiah is writing first to *his people* in *his time* and secondly to those of us living *now*. To his people, he was speaking directly to the acts of their past that did everything *but* bring honor to God. To sum it up, they worshiped, served, sacrificed to, and adored other gods.

Their everyday behavior matched that disobedience. Although this is true, Isaiah writes that through the promise of Christ, they could forget the shame of their youth.

And through faith in Christ, we can do the same.

I look back at the sins of my past, at the "shame of my youth," and honestly, most of it seems unforgivable. In my own heart, these sins seem so strong, as if they could never be forgotten, not by me and certainly not by God.

But Isaiah writes that all of our shame will be forgotten; that all of it will be lost. This word implies that every bit of significance found in our shameful acts, and every bit of pain and anger that it caused God, will *vanish*.

All of my disobedience was cleansed.

The shame of our youth, the disgusting sins of our past, every act that was done, and all the stuff that makes our stomachs cringe is forgiven and no more. And I am talking about all of it.

The freeing aspect of this truth is that apart from this shame, we can victoriously and obediently stand in Christ. If the sins of our past are vanished and our future is forever with Christ, then we can focus our attention on today.

We can obey Him today.

If those sins are forgotten, then it leaves us with no reason to go back to them. Our Redeemer is here, alive, and longing to work through us now.

The Reproach of Our Widowhood

But that is not all. There are more promises to uncover.

Isaiah writes that all of Israel will forget the *"reproach of their widowhood."* In Isaiah's day, a barren widow was something disgraceful. Fertility and motherhood was prized and honored. Women saw this as their purpose and their way to bring meaning to their lives and their world.

But a barren woman felt disgraced. She was seen as having no purpose. Therefore, she constantly felt scorn from the world around her. She could bear nothing; no life came from her.

And Israel (and you and I) were once like this.

Because of the fall, all of humanity lost the ability to truly bring life to the world. We became barren. We lived without purpose and meaning, doing everything *but* bearing the fruit we were destined to produce. In our shame, we felt the scorn of the world telling us all that we did wrong.

Nothing meaningful or fruitful came from us. Life felt lifeless.

But our Husband, our Maker, our Redeemer came back for us. He took us back, out of that disgrace and away from the taunting voices of the world and our enemy.

Because of Christ, we are now above every reproach and above every lie. Our life is not defined by what we lost because of the Fall, but by what we gained because of Christ.

Think about that.

Your life is defined by what you gained in Christ: Him.

We are His bride. With Him, we are given the ability to stand blameless and pure. And with Him, we are given the ability to bear much fruit. Now alive, we can bring about life.

Life as Servants

What I love about the ending of chapter 54 is that Isaiah suddenly shifts his word choice. In an instant, the word "Servant" becomes plural. Instead of Servant, it now reads "servants."

And from this point on, Jesus is no longer separated from the people that He came to save. The Servant of the Lord is now one with the "servants of the Lord."

What He has, He has given to us.

We are now Kingdom heirs.

> "No weapon forged against you will prevail, and you will refute every tongue that accuses you. This is the heritage of the servants of the LORD, and this is their vindication from Me," declares the LORD.
>
> -Isaiah 54:17

These are words that the Lord declares, commands, and shouts over us. With all of His authority, the epitome of ALL authority, He says that no accusation can be held against us.

We are His servants, one with His Servant.

Before Christ, all we could do was sin and be ashamed of it. But now, in Christ, we will never be anything less than perfect, holy, and righteous. We now have the power to choose holiness and obedience.

In the New Testament, Paul proclaims that we are actually servants of righteousness, a people who are continually made new by our Lord (Romans 6:18). He writes that we were of no benefit when living ashamed, but now we get our benefits from Christ; those being both sanctification and eternal life (21-22).

Literally nothing that Satan can do or say will hold ground against us. As servants of righteousness, we can refute the devil and his demons, calling them out as evil.

For in Christ, we are above all reproach and above all shame.

Like a new bride reverently holding onto her groom, we now stand as one with Christ. And like a new bride shining brightly in her white dress, we now stand perfect and blameless.

The eternal treasure that is inside of us is powerfully seen when we understand His presence with us. The truth of the life we now live should completely drown out the lies of Satan. Although he works persistently, with Christ, we can refute and silence his accusing tongue.

Being more than clay, we can live unashamed.

QUESTIONS FOR REFLECTION

1. What were/are your thoughts when you read: "You are no longer sinful; you are complete; perfect.

2. Reread Romans 8:35-39. If you are completely honest with yourself, are their aspects of this passage that are hard for you to believe? If so, what?

3. Reread Isaiah 54:4-5. These two verses make many promises. Write down the promise(s) that stand out to you. Do you feel like this promise is true in your life? Why or why not?

4. As servants of the Lord, we are called to live above Satan's accusations. Spend some time in Romans 6 discovering what it means for you to be a servant of righteousness.

PART 3

LIVING UNASHAMED

CHAPTER 9

THE BLAMELESS LIFE

*"Great was thy grace in commanding me to
come hand in hand with thee to the Father…
in giving me the Spirit as teacher, guide,
power, that I may live repenting of sin,
conquer Satan, find victory in life."*
-Puritan Prayer on Victory

Satan approaches the Lord…

It's a weird and unfamiliar way to start off a story, but please humor me by rolling with it.

On this particular day, we see Satan approaching God.

Looking down at him, the Lord Almighty speaks, "Where have you come from?" Being confused by the question, Satan answers, "From roaming through the earth and walking up and down it."

Under his breath is a hint of rude humor – as if this Liar is trying to imply to God that it is he who rules all of the earth: *I can walk up and down, marking my territory, because it is all mine… not Yours.*

But in confidence, complete confidence, the Lord continues:

"Have you considered my servant here?"

As He speaks, the Lord points toward a human, directing Satan's attention off of what he thinks is his and onto someone that is clearly not his.

"No one on earth can compare," the Lord says to His enemy, "this servant is blameless and upright, an obedient follower who fears Me and shuns evil."

Satan's stomach churns.

"This servant has no reason to not fear You," he insists. "You have placed a barrier of protection around him and blessed his work," says the Accuser, "But if You stretch out Your hand, take away all that he has, and make his life go spiraling down, then he will curse Your face."

"Very well," the Lord replies, "Everything that this servant has is in your power, but you may not lay a finger on him. For this is My servant."

"I can do whatever I wish?" says the Accuser, his mind flowing with a list full of schemes and lures that he has been waiting to use.

"Everything that this servant has is in your power," says the Lord again, "But you may not lay a finger on him." And with a stern voice, the same voice that created the whole of creation, He repeats: "For this is *My* servant."

After this, Satan leaves the presence of the Lord.

THE POWER OF THE BLAMELESS

For some of you, the previous story sounds *very* familiar.

In fact, for the most part, this is the same dialogue that is found in the first chapter of the book of Job. What may confuse many of you, however, is why I did not include Job's name in the account at all.

Maybe this particular Bible story is one of your favorites, so you, having memorized every bit of it, were waiting to read "my servant *Job*," only to discover that it was not there.

You see, I did not include Job's name in this account because I was not, in any way, writing about Job. The truth is the servant that I am writing about, without a doubt, is both you and me.

The story above is our story.

Now, I am not saying this is the exact way that God and Satan communicate. But the inclusion of this little conversation does seem to give us a peek into what is going on in the spiritual realm around us.

Satan, the ruler of the earth, the father of the "world," thinks that he owns everything in it. But to his demise, this thought is nothing but a lie. In fact, all of creation is under the feet of an amazing God. And whether Satan wants to agree with this or not, there are also thousands of servants who are no longer his.

They are all the servants of righteousness.

They are all followers of the Living Lord.

And, like Job, they are all blameless and upright. Nothing on earth can compare with the servants of the Lord. As we uncovered in the last chapter, we are these servants. But with complete confidence, God allows Satan to work around us.

This thought is hard to grasp. Even though I do not intend to try to make complete sense of, it seems as if Satan can do nothing without God allowing him. In the Lord's supreme control, He allows Satan to work against Him; to try and misuse our free will.

We can spend a whole chapter uncovering this, but a pursuit like this actually takes our eyes off the beauty of this thought. Yes, God does allow Satan to work around us; to lie to us. But God allows Satan to work around us because He is *confident* in us.

When Satan sees humanity, he sees a group of two-legged animals that are created in the image of his ultimate "Enemy." To him, we are worthless, disgusting, and vile. He sees no point in God creating, sustaining, let alone loving us.

But when God, our Beloved Creator, sees us, He sees His prized creation being forever united with His Son. Because of this, when God sees us, He sees overcomers. Just as His Son overcame death, we can overcome. In fact, the very power that raised Christ from the dead is inside of each and every believer. It is the very treasure inside of each of us.

Like a proud Father watching his child ride a bike for the first time, God looks at us with righteous pride. Because of His Son, He finds His glory and honor in us.

So God allows Satan to work around us and to lie to us because He is confident in *who* we are. He is confident that we will overcome. And He is confident that His glory will ultimately be seen and proclaimed through us.

In fact, the very reason that God allowed Satan to torment Job was because God knew that Job would be faithful through all of it. God *knew* that Job could persevere and glorify Him through all of it.

For every ounce of Job's consistent faith was a proclamation of how great God was and still is. And every ounce of Job's faith was a proclamation of what was not and will never be Satan's.

And if you've read the story of Job, you know that Satan hit him with some heavy attacks. He lost everything; his work, his animals, his family, and his health. Every physical hit was accompanied with a spiritual one. Satan aimed at damaging his "seen" life so much that it would get him to forget the God who was throughout the unseen.

But every time Job proved his consistent faithfulness—every time he continued to put his thoughts on the Lord—he silenced the

Accuser's lies. He chose to see every outer issue as a way to proclaim God's greatness.

And this is the same with us.

God is confident in us as overcomers and He knows that we will, through His power, overcome the lies of the devil. Although we have dozens of scars, dents, and cracks throughout our life, it is through them that God's greatness shines the best.

In the second letter to the Corinthian church, Paul reminds them and us that Jesus has given His authority to His followers. In fact, Paul states that Jesus has "committed to us" a powerful "message of reconciliation," one that restores the world (chapter 5).

Satan is helpless when that message is proclaimed.

When we remain faithful, the truth of Satan's loss is seen completely. And when we remain faithful, the reality of our God's greatness is proclaimed in and through us. Our obedience, just like Jesus' obedience, makes a public spectacle of Satan and his tactics.

Satan can exhaust his resources on us, but every hit only allows God's treasure to be seen in us more and more vividly. All we must do is remain faithful and obedient.

But it is important to remember that faithfulness and obedience are learned over time; living an unashamed life is a journey. Therefore, it is normal to feel as if you have not "made it there" or "obtained it" yet. Although this is true, when God looks at us, He does not just see us where we once were or where we are now, but He sees a full picture—where we've been, where we are now, and where we will be.

In His eyes, we are overcomers.

For inside all believers is the Spirit of God. Even now, He is at work in us to help bring about both the faithfulness and obedience needed to overcome Satan's shameful lies.

God knows that it is our gradual acts of faith and obedience that can ruin the work of His enemy. Although you may feel far from a life of obedience right now, that will not always be the case. The Lord promises that we will overcome, and unlike our wavering faithfulness, His is eternal.

With that said, I call you to no longer be victimized by Satan's lies. It is normal to not feel blameless, it is normal to not feel like an overcomer, and it is normal to feel helpless. But the truth is that you are blameless, you are an overcomer, and you certainly are not helpless when hidden in Jesus Christ.

PRACTICAL STEPS

The truths above are what lead us toward taking the much-needed steps out of being victimized by shame and into being victorious with Christ. My hope is that even now you are being strengthened by who you really are in reality. It is in this strength that we can choose obedience and battle our enemy.

You see, if all of this, every chapter that you have read previously, is left in this book, then your battle with shame will never seem to end. Although the truth of who we are in Christ is important to understand, it will prove to be *nothing* if our actions do not proclaim that we truly believe it. With that said, you will discover a difference between these next few chapters and the ones that you have already read.

It is here that we will take God's truth of who we are in Him and let our lives be shaped and transformed by it.

This last section is full of practical application.

Because we are new, holy, and righteous through Christ, we have the ability to live a life free of shame; a life that is blameless and obedient. We are, as Peter states, participators in God's divine nature. But he continues:

> For this reason, make every effort to add to your faith goodness; and to goodness, knowledge; and to knowledge, self-control; and to self-control, perseverance; and to perseverance, godliness; and to godliness; brotherly kindness; and to brotherly kindness, love. For if you possess these qualities in increasing measure, they will keep you from being ineffective and unproductive in your knowledge of our Lord Jesus Christ.
>
> - 2 Peter 1: 5-8

Knowledge is important, but knowledge should always lead you toward growing in self-control, perseverance, godliness, mutual affection, and ultimately love. In our battle with shame, truth is only powerful if we seek these qualities as well. Halting at truth will only give us an ineffective and unproductive faith.

Therefore, I challenge both you and myself.

With the help of these upcoming chapters, we will take the truths that were previously read, whether they were new to our minds or not, and apply them genuinely to our lives.

Because shame begins with a lie and ends with a habit of disobedience, we will start off by looking inward, deep within our hearts, to discover our believed lies.

And as we progress, we will focus outwardly on our actions and the community around us.

You must remember that shame is a direct threat against our spiritual journey. So even now, do not let it withdraw you from what is coming up next.

These chapters will provide ways to intentionally work through your shame. With that said, some of the areas of application may seem challenging, time consuming, or just plain "awkward." It is up to you to step up and push yourself through them.

Through it all, however, know that you are not alone. In fact, our spiritual journey out from under Satan's lies is *never* to be done alone. If you start to feel that way, find someone to do these practical chapters with; someone that will walk through them with you.

But more than anything else, in order to fight shame you must learn to lean on the truths that God proclaims over us. No matter how many times you have read it, you may have to go back to the previous chapters and re-read who God says you are.

This is because only truth will beat the shameful lies of Satan.

With that said, please enjoy the next section. And together we can work toward practically fighting shame and realizing that we are so much more than clay.

QUESTIONS FOR REFLECTION

1. What came to mind as you were compared to Job, a servant who is "blameless and upright, an obedient follower who fears God and shuns evil?"

2. How does it make you feel to know that God is confident in you?

3. Your faithfulness silences Satan. Write down some raw thoughts and feelings that are evoked when reading that statement.

4. Take this time and pray for this next section of application.

Chapter 10

Searching Deep

Search me, God, and know my heart;
test me and know my anxious thoughts.
See if there is any offensive way in me,
and lead me in the way everlasting.
- Psalm 139: 23-24

"Greg, what do you think is the *real* issue?"

"Well…I don't know," I said thoughtfully.

This situation, like many before, had me sitting across from my mentor, searching deep for an answer to give him. In that moment, the Greg sitting there was a nasty product of two solid months of stress, pressure, and failure. I was wide-eyed and sleep deprived.

"Well, then talk it out," he stated with a reassuring voice.

And after a deep breath, I spent the next hour and a half vomiting up words and emotions. Although this time of introspection was difficult to go through, it allowed me to discover a lie burrowed deep in my heart, something that I had chosen to believe. Like all lies, it began to drastically affect my life, my marriage, and my relationship with God.

"I just feel like I have to be better, like my life does not have meaning unless I perform right—unless I prove myself. But right now I have nothing to prove, it seems like I just keep failing; that I am not good enough."

As I sat and spilled out my shame, I finally uncovered that I had, and still have today, an overwhelming *need* and desire to be perfect. I felt that I was consistently missing the mark, constantly coming up short, and every bit of it was making me hit a rock solid wall of failure and shame.

"Greg," my mentor said calmly.

I remember lifting up my head and looking into his eyes.

"In that last statement," he continued, "You said a complete lie… but in that last statement you also said a truth."

Of course this instantly confused me.

He continued, "The lie that you are believing is that you *have* to strive in order to have meaning. That in order for you to matter, you have to be 'perfect'… The truth that you expressed, that's easy. You have nothing to prove."

Like waves rolling over and over in the sea, his words, my own words, came crashing through my mind. But this time, they had a new meaning attached to them.

I had, and I still have, nothing to prove.

To this very day, I must remind myself of the implications of that truth. Without that reminder, I end up right back in that place of shame and failure. I do not have to strive for perfection; for I have nothing to prove.

What amazes me, however, is that every one of our believed lies are swarming around an ounce of truth. Yes, I have nothing to prove because of Christ's work, but the lie of needing to be the best, to be perfect, can turn that positive truth into something that can lead straight toward shame.

I will never reach that false view of perfection, and Satan knows this. So he cleverly twists the truth of me having nothing to prove because of Christ's work, into me having nothing to prove because I am not good enough, because I am "crap."

He always will team up his lies with a truth. But in order to discover the beautiful weight of those truths, we must uncover and pull apart the lies that our hearts have believed all this time.

I would have never moved past that state of shame if I was not challenged to search deep for the real problem. On the surface, the issue was that I was angry, bitter, and upset at myself. Although this is true, under those emotions was my core lie.

It was what fed my actions; my stressed-out and selfish actions.

We all need to pull open our feelings and look inward for the false belief that is in control of them. Therefore, this chapter is all about introspection, all about *searching deep* inside of our hearts.

Like my mentor, I ask you this simple question:

What do you think is the *real* issue, the *real* reason that your life has shame?

THE LOOKS OF SHAME

Because I know that a question like this is hard to answer, I have decided to provide you with some help. Below, you will find five major "looks of shame" to read through. They are the common characteristics that express our inner shame; the outward display of our believed lies.

I say the word "major" because these are just five of the *many* ways that our shame surfaces. But these five are definitely real and prevalent in our lives.

As you read, you will discover that each one will be personified by a true story. These are real people, much like you and me, who encounter shame but have chosen to battle and endure through it.

Although this chapter is lengthier than many of the others before it, do not let that intimidate you from intentionally reading and searching for your own look of shame. As you read along, you may also discover that one, two, three, or maybe even all of them sound like you. If so, do not worry. We all, at some level, struggle in these various areas.

So know that you are not alone.

In fact, right now I challenge you to realize God's hand in this time of introspection. He is the Searcher of our hearts. Even though this is true, He longs to do this as one with us; that as He searches our innermost parts, we, ourselves, are searching them as well.

So before you continue, take a short break and ask the Lord for help as you read through these descriptions. Ask Him to make known your lie; to lead you along His path.

> Search me, God, and know my heart; test me and know
> my anxious thoughts. See if there is any offensive way
> in me, and lead me in the way everlasting.
>   - Psalm 139: 23-24

Without Him, you will discover nothing.

But with His help, I fully believe that you will be guided away from the enemy's lies and into the Lord's beautiful truth.

Know that He is present and eager to move in your heart.

The Prisoners of the Past

The training process for the United States Marine Corps does not, in any way, prepare one for the spiritual warfare felt when stationed overseas. Although I cannot imagine the intensity of this, a very dear friend of mine experienced it firsthand.

When I first met him, I had no idea of the amount of shame and guilt that weighed upon his heart from his past.

When entering into the Marines, he took with him a solid list of Christian morals, ones that carried him through many temptations. But as time passed, the burden of continually stepping out alone became heavier and heavier to bear.

Slowly, after being drained by the world around him, he became a target for the lures and temptations of the sex industry. One night the constant pressure from his fellow marines became too much, leading him to pay for his first prostitute.

I can remember the shame in his voice when he initially told me of this aspect of his past. Although he now wishes that it had stopped with that first experience, the war continued within him, taking him deeper and deeper into that sin.

His experiences overseas built up inside of him such a deep sense of guilt and regret. He could not separate the individual acts of sex from his own image of himself. And as shame always does, it caused him to view himself as something disgusting and vile.

But this Marine who told me his experiences was nowhere close to being disgusting or vile. In front of me was a man of integrity, one that was already being used by God regardless of the memories and sins that he carried with him.

But he, like many of us, had become a "Prisoner of the Past."

He allowed the dark shadows of what he had done, the acts that *he* committed, to take power over the man that he was in Christ—thus transforming his overall identity.

Although you may have never experienced this Marine's specific shame, the fact is that many of these feelings may hit very close to home for you. If so, you are a Prisoner of the Past.

Through Satan's deception, you have allowed the sins of your past to control you in the now. You have allowed them to still have power in your hearts.

We each do this by continually reminding ourselves of the people *we* hurt, of the things that *we* destroyed, and of the innocence, whether our own or others, that *we* lost or took. As these thoughts run through our minds, we build up a prison around ourselves and place our own chains on either wrist.

We become Prisoners of the Past because we hold ourselves back from the grace given to us on the cross.

Yes, sin and disobedience should be punished.

But we are to never be the ones who try to punish it. In fact, in the moments where we try, we lack the clarity needed to separate our sinful acts from who we are now.

So every time we look upon our sins with judgment, we look upon *ourselves* with judgment. And without even realizing it, we have become an easy target for shame.

But we should not, and cannot, punish sin.

Jesus, the only one for the job, already did just that.

As a previous prisoner myself, one of the best and most compelling challenges that the Lord gave me was this:

> I should – *you* should – never, at any time, look upon sin without seeing it through the work that Jesus already did on the cross.

This means that every time I am reminded of an act that I have done in the past, whether through a painful memory, old habitual thoughts, or a terrible nightmare, I must choose to see it paid for on the cross.

Truthfully, this challenge is very difficult to make a habit. But I have found that the freedom it extends is eternal. If you are a Prisoner of the Past, do not fret. Although I leave you with this challenge, know that I have a whole chapter coming up next on how to live it out.

The Future Pursuer

In order to escape the memories of the past, he has a tendency to look ahead, ready for what is next. Another dear friend of mine struggles with being a "Future Pursuer."

Like many of us, he has a past that he is not so proud of. But instead of staying imprisoned by it, his attention has been drawn forward at what he could be, at what he *should* be.

> I should be a great man.
> I should be successful.
> I should be a provider.
> I should be a leader.

And without realizing it, he has attached on each of these "shoulds" a definition that can only be met in the future:

> *I will be a great man when my sin is over.*
> *I will be successful when I have a steady job.*
> *I will be a provider when I have a family.*
> *I will be a leader when I am married.*

As the famous therapists Alfred Adler and Albert Ellis describe, he has a strong problem with "shoulding on" himself.

Yes, you can read it again: "shoulding on" himself.

So, in order to be what he *should* be in the future, he pursues a present path that will reach, in his view, each of those *shoulds*. The problem with this is that when pursuing future shoulds, he forgets the man who he already is in Christ.

His believed lie is that he is not good enough now. That he has not "met the mark" *yet*; that he is still incomplete. And every day that he believes this, he feels the shame of not being what he should be.

In fact, if Satan can get him to consider himself as incomplete, then he is much more inclined to act like someone incomplete; he's much more likely to habitually sin.

In a conversation with him, realization of this came about:

"Greg, I look to the future for everything. I even feel like my sins will not be dealt with until then, that I will not be complete until later in life. But when I think like that, I choose to fall into sin now."

I know that his realization may seem simple, but the very reason that many of us keep falling into sin is because we still consider ourselves incomplete. But in Christ, my friend has already met the mark and has been made complete; we have been made complete.

I am not saying that we do not need to grow, to change, and to develop in Christ. In fact, if you remember in the Garden of Eden, both Adam and Eve were given tasks that would both develop and grow them in perfection.

They were made complete, but were made to grow in that completeness. And the same is true for us.

But a Future Pursuer forgets this important truth. In their minds, they will only *be* what they should be when _____ happens. When they graduate high school, complete their degree plan, get the best paying job, buy their first house, get married, have kids, and have a yard with a dog.

But these pursuits distract us from daily pursuing Christ.

And like my friend, nothing will ever seem to make our original "shoulds" come true. The day that he gets a steady job will be the day that his definition of success changes to something greater; something that he cannot yet meet. And once again, he will pursue that new future should.

And the same is true for all of us future pursuers.

On a daily basis, we need to recognize the work that Jesus did to make us complete and whole *now*.

Because we are one with him, we are good enough.

And it is when my friend sees himself as complete that he begins to act out in that completeness each and every day. It is then when he begins to realize not what he should be, but what he is.

Because he is a great man. He is successful. He is a provider. And He is a leader. The crazy truth is God shines each of these traits brightly through him, and everyone around him knows it... except him.

So for every Future Pursuer out there, take a moment, remind yourself of who you presently are in Christ, and take every "should" captive. Focusing on the future only distracts us from the acts of completeness that we were made to do *now*.

The Heavy Plater

Teamed up nicely with the Future Pursuer is the Heavy Plater. Although I could gladly point my finger at a number of people in my life who align with this trait, the person that most personifies it right now...is me.

The Heavy Plater believes that significance is equivalent to a great amount of responsibilities. Although they will not outwardly state this, deep down they believe that their life matters *only* when they have a lot to do.

For the past few weeks of my life, I completely exemplified that lie. The saddest thing is that I did not even realize it until this last weekend. But realization came as I looked upon the angry, bitter, prideful, and selfish pig that I had been.

For weeks, I *had* to do it all. I *had* to be the best pastor with the best sermons. I *had* to paint our new house. I *had* to get everything moved in. I *had* to fix our car. I *had* to mow the lawn. And I *had* be everything and do everything that I *thought* my pregnant wife needed for me to be and do.

And most importantly, I *had* to do it all by myself.

Upon my shoulders, I placed every bit of responsibility that I possibly could. In my mind, it made me seem *better*, because I could handle it all.

But oh, did that come crashing down. For those of you who tend to be Heavy Platers, know that the crash always comes at some point.

It is the moment when all of our responsibilities clearly become too much for us to handle. It is the moment that we crack and things begin to fall apart. And it is the moment that our biggest fear, that we are complete failures, hits us straight in the face.

My crash happened while I was attempting to change the oil in our car. I have never been the best handy-man, but changing the oil had never been a problem for me before. But in my overly-responsible, Heavy-Plated self, I made this task much harder than it should have been.

After breaking the filter, completely stripping the oil plug, and spilling oil all over my driveway, I realized that I could not do it alone.

Instantly, I crashed. I was angry and completely upset that I could not do it without needing help.

In that moment, I turned into a huffy, puffy four-year-old who just realized that he could not tie a shoe on his own.

Much like the four-year-old, I felt like a complete failure.

But this was much deeper to me than not being able to change the oil filter. In fact, when I could not do something that I thought I *had* to do, my sense of significance was questioned.

When our responsibilities crash and become too much to handle, our feelings of significance are drastically lowered. And in order for us to feel significant again, we feel like we *have* to do more. This only allows the cycle of shame to continue.

Significance, however, is not found in what we do or in the things that we are in charge of. If the Heavy Plater ever wants to break the cycle, that is the first thing that they must realize.

The lies of Satan can truly trip us up, making us believe that the only way to not feel shame is to try harder—to do more.

But true significance is found through surrender.

This means that our significance in Christ was found the *moment* that we surrendered our whole self to Him and continues each and every time that we surrender more of ourselves.

So for all of you Heavy Platers out there, know that Jesus Christ already took the plate, the "cup" of our sins, to the cross. He did it all so that the only thing left for us to do is surrender our all. So true significance is only found through surrender.

Responsibilities, by any means, are not bad. In fact, we are given responsibilities as opportunities to shine who Jesus is. But when I let my responsibilities fuel my feeling of significance, I take away every bit of significance that could and should be given to Jesus.

As a Heavy Plater, I must separate myself from both my to-do list and each responsibility that I possess. For me, this is done every time that I surrender them to God's will and desire.

And you must do the same.

It is then that we can show who Christ is; our Savior who has already made us worthy, significant, and able.

The Constant Comparer

The other night, my wife broke down.

The season that we are currently in is one of complete transition. With that said, I cannot adequately describe the amount of change that has happened during these past eight months.

In that short time, Kate and I became expectant parents of twins, I got hired on as a new Student Pastor, and we became brand new homeowners. Although each of these changes are complete blessings, their combined weight has been difficult to manage.

And the other night, my wife wanted out.

The chaos of this season got her desiring the "simple" life that we once had. She wanted to be free from the weight of our new responsibilities by having the life of eight months ago; a life that she felt was better than the one in reality.

And in her break down, I discovered that she had been harboring these feelings for months.

In her mind, she had constructed a past that was so much "prettier" than our present. In her view, it was the life that she wanted so desperately. Like many of us, my wonderful wife became tricked into taking on the role of a "Constant Comparer."

Being distracted by something outside of themselves, the Constant Comparer longs for something more, something better. As they fixate on what they do not have, they involuntarily make way for shame to penetrate their heart.

Whether it is a prettier face, a better job, cooler clothes, a slimmer body, a "holier" life, or a past situation like my wife, we all find things to which we compare our current reality.

Although tempting, *comparison always breeds discontentment.*

But this discontentment with who we are or where we are is nothing but a distraction from Satan. When he can hold our attention on what we don't have, he can keep us from realizing all the grace and blessings that we do have.

Although that concept is simple, the complex part is what is happening under the surface in our heart.

The comparer's heart becomes full of lies, telling them that they are not good enough without _____. This lie makes them believe that they are missing something because they do not have "it" or cannot do "it."

As this lie grows, their built up anger and resentment can lessen their view of their own God-given potential. Not only this, but the Constant Comparer may have a hard time truly loving themselves and others.

The more that I compare myself, the more I start resenting those who may seem to be more gifted than I am. This bitter resentment blocks my ability to extend genuine love to both those individuals and myself.

When our attention is off of the grace and blessings of life, we miss seeing God. Our discontentment distracts us from thankfulness and the peace that comes with it.

For God is in reality. In fact, God *is* reality.

When my wife and I compare our lives with how we wish they were, we create a fantasy life.

Think about it.

Every time that you imagine yourself having *that* body, or *that* voice, or *that* job, or *that* life, you are creating a reality that is not true. And to be honest, God is not in that reality, that reality is man-made, not God-made.

The "you" that He created, that He desires for you to be, is the one that you are now. Even though we have a hard time believing it, He loves and accepts us as we are now.

His truth tells us that He came into the world so that we would have life and life to the fullest (John 10:10). That is not the life that we wish we had in our fantasies, but the life that we do have. And if you are in Christ, then the life to the fullest that you do have is one full of grace and blessings and one that you are choosing not to see.

Constant Comparers, you must realize that you—who you are presently—are already good enough. Give over to God those false realities that you long for, and seek the grace and blessings that you have in reality now.

My wife had to realize and do this herself. The life that she wanted, the life of eight months ago, was without God. Although it does not make sense and certainly does not feel like it, the place where we are currently is the place that God wants us to be. My wife had to rely on and be thankful for the promise that God is *here*, a truth that is already better than her fantasy life without Him.

You see, the best medicine for a Constant Comparer is genuine thankfulness. Every bit of discontentment vanishes when one is truly thankful for what they have.

Because of this, my wife and I reminded ourselves of each and every blessing that the Lord has given us in our *real* life. In the list was every person and experience that we would have never encountered without going through this transitioning season.

And I leave you with that same charge.

If you struggle with comparing yourself, then set this book aside and compile a list of every blessing that is in your present reality. They are there, under the thick layers of discontentment that you have paved.

The Approval Addict

Under a boulder of other people's opinions, you can find the "Approval Addict." The humbling truth is that all of us have portions of this addiction somewhere inside of our hearts. We all, in our own way, want to be liked and known by others.

But for the Approval Addict, this desire finds itself at the heart of many of their decisions.

A very close friend of mine has a past of approval addiction. Although it has crept into most areas of his life, his discovery of this "look of shame" came about recently.

In a very personal and tangible way, God revealed to him his life-long need to be approved by others. It started about a year ago when he felt a strong push toward ending a healthy dating relationship with his best friend.

The confusing part for both him and all of those around him was the *why*. There were no issues, no problems, and no disagreements anywhere in the relationship. On the outside, all was great.

But after sitting in this confusion for a while, he felt God's pressure more and more. Finally, this brought him to a place of obedience, a place that many of his closest friends saw as insanity. One day, he ended the relationship.

Although it was a tough and stressful time for him, he chose to act in faith. But it was not until months later that God chose to disclose the *why* to him.

You see, in that relationship, he thrived on her words of affirmation. Being both a lovable and encouraging person, she continually fed something inside of him that wanted approval.

Without realizing it, she became his source of meaning, allowing aspects of his worth to be found in her uplifting words. Instead of him giving needed attention to the wounds and insecurities deep within his heart, he found a personal "bandage" who seemed to cover them up for him.

At the heart of the Approval Addict is a longing, a deep desire, to be important, needed, and wanted by everyone around them. One of the biggest sources of fuel for this pursuit is the belief that without others' approval, they are not important, needed, or wanted.

So they seek the world's attention, hoping that it will see them as better than they see themselves. "If other people think that I am beautiful, then maybe I will be beautiful"…or… "If my boss sees me as important, maybe that means I actually am important."

This need for attention has us fluffing up our lives through social media, wearing clothes that may be just a little too revealing, and acting overly confident in our friend circles.

We want approval anywhere that we can get it.

But under these facades are hearts that do not feel good enough. Over time, they have become chained into believing that worth is only found through the validation of others.

The truth, however, is that we become controlled by the things that we seek approval from.

Let me say that again.

We put ourselves under the control of everything or everyone that we seek attention and approval from. Without realizing it, we blindly hand over the reins of our lives to those who we want to please.

"I will be what you want me to be…."

And soon, the world of social media becomes our god, the attention that we gain with our body brings us to people who demand more, and our friends become dictators of our lives.

But this is not God's plan for us. Because we are one with Christ, we are forever approved. In fact, the biblical word for that is "justified."

Think of a courtroom where you are on trial. Deep down, you know of everything that you have done. And deep down, you know that you should be punished for every bit of it.

But because you gave your life to Christ, you are no longer seen alone in that courtroom. With you is Jesus himself. Because of Him, you are good enough. Because of Him, we have forever been approved by God.

We are justified. Therefore, we seek to please God only.

Paul writes this to the Galatian church:

> Am I now trying to win the approval of men, or of God? Or am I trying to please men? If I were still trying to please men, I would not be a servant of Christ.
>
> - Galatians 1:10

Paul understood that those we seek to please end up controlling us. This is why he states that he is a servant of Christ. His goal is not to be approved by men but to constantly aim at pleasing his Heavenly Father.

This should be our aim as well.

It is my hope that you are beginning to realize the things or the people that you seek approval from. The fact is that every time you regard their approval as important, then you disregard the approval of your Heavenly Father.

What you need is to tangibly take away the reins that you have given to that thing or that person and give them back to God. Remember that you are His servant, not the world's.

To my lifelong friend, that meant ending a relationship that seemed healthy from the outside. To you, it will look different.

But the heart of it is always the same.

By taking away the reins, you are destroying the idols, the gods in your life that give you temporary meaning, and gladly placing them at the feet of your one true God. For He is the One that gives you eternal meaning. To Him, you are already important, needed, and wanted.

A Perfect Realization

Although I have given only five "looks of shame," my hope and prayer is that at least one of these has connected deeply with you.

If not, seek God and ask Him to give you clarity to the lies that you have chosen to believe.

They are there.

But for all of us, one thing that I have discovered through much of my studying is how closely related shame is with perfectionism. In fact, many studies have been recorded on how the need or pursuit to be "perfect" can both initiate and sustain our feelings of shame.

As you know, I included the quotation marks because there is a large contrast between humanity's "perfect" and God's perfect.

But if you think back, I did not include the "Perfect Pursuer" as one of the looks of shame. This is because I believe that Satan teams up every one of our believed lies with this pursuit. In fact, my story at the very beginning of this chapter displays just that.

You see, the Prisoner of the Past is unforgiving of themselves because they are not "perfect," the Future Pursuer longs for a day when they will be "perfect," the Heavy-Plater's definition of significance is teamed with their definition of "perfection," the Constant Comparer desires the "perfect" life of others, and the Approval Addict wants to be seen by others as "perfect."

All of our lies are connected with perfectionism.

I would even say that this is one of the major *truths* onto which Satan attaches his lies.

Let me explain.

In all of us, there is a deep need for something to be fixed. We know, without a shadow of doubt, that we lost something. And without an explanation, we know that it was perfection; that is, fullness and completeness.

Because this was lost, we naturally long for it once again. But this pursuit is not bad. It is a true and *righteous* aspect of who we are. For God created us to long for that completion. It is in this search for fullness that we initially discover God's love.

This is because the only place to find perfection is in God's perfect Son. Yet every day, we struggle with seeking and pursuing it elsewhere. This must end. No matter what your believed lies or your looks of shame may be, separate them from your pursuit of perfection; your pursuit of completeness.

It is when Satan no longer taints this pursuit that we are able to clearly see the source of perfection being Jesus Christ. In Him we find forgiveness, significance, and approval.

So I urge you, pursue true perfection; pursue Jesus. For when you do, the lies of Satan will lose their grip.

QUESTIONS FOR REFLECTION

1. Have you been truly honest with yourself while reading this chapter? If not, meditate over Psalm 139:23-24 and read the looks of shame again.

2. What look(s) of shame are common for you? Explain how.

3. What can you do this week to intentionally fight those looks of shame?

4. Take a moment to ponder the redeeming grace given to you to help you overcome your look of shame.

5. In what areas of your life do you strive for perfection? How has this hurt your pursuit of Jesus?

CHAPTER 11

GRACING OURSELVES

"I have learned, that the person I have to ask for
forgiveness from the most is: myself. You must love yourself.
You have to forgive yourself, every day, whenever you
remember a shortcoming, a flaw; you have to tell yourself
"That's just fine"…Because that's what love is."
- C. JoyBell C.

The other day I stumbled across an article about the intensive counseling given to American criminals. Apparently they go through a long series of sessions aimed at correcting both their thoughts and behavior patterns.

If you're like me, this little fact may come as no shock at all. It seems like common sense for correctional facilities to provide some type of correction.

But as I read on, something in the article caught my attention. Out of the number of different correctional therapies, the one that has proven most effective in the long run is centered on self-forgiveness; getting the criminals to choose to forgive themselves.

Research gives two main reasons for this.

The first is that *past forgiveness changes future decisions*. This study revealed that the self-forgiven offenders were less likely to make negative decisions in their present because they truly forgave their negative decisions of the past.

Without the practice of self-forgiveness, other offenders were left trapped in a viewpoint that labeled themselves as nothing more than offenders. Because of this, their behaviors were continually aligned with that viewpoint.

If you see yourself as a criminal, you will most likely act like a criminal.

Once forgiven, however, they were able to see themselves as more than troublemakers, allowing their behavior to now match this newfound identity.

The second finding revealed that the *self-forgiveness produces empathy and love for others.* Unlike ever before, the criminals in this study were able to seek reconciliation for their wrongdoings; even from their victims. Self-forgiveness led them to true healing.

This is powerful stuff.

These convicted criminals began overcoming the shame of their crimes through discovering something called grace.

But why do I start out with this?

Maybe you would never label yourself as "destructive" as a murderer or sexual offender, but the fact is that both you and I could and should be labeled as lawbreakers. Our anger labels us as murderers, our lust places us as sexual offenders, and our envy and jealousy make us thieves.

These are not my words; they are Jesus' in Matthew 5.

We all, without a doubt, should be labeled lawbreakers. And with lawbreaking comes shame and punishment. Although this is true, I am sure that you know by now that we are not what we should be. Nor are we treated as we should be treated.

This is because we have become unashamed by God's grace.

But the problem is that even though we have His grace, even though we have newness, we still choose to limit ourselves from it. This is done through us constantly *unforgiving ourselves.*

Just like an inmate, our unforgiveness causes us to become prisoners of our shame, locking us into our habitual negative thoughts and behaviors. But just like an inmate, the only way out, the only way to receive restoration and "correction," is through continually gracing ourselves.

But first, we must do some de-weeding.

SEEDS OF UNFORGIVENESS

I do not know if you have ever noticed this, but nowhere in Wal-Mart, Lowes, or any other home and garden store, can you find weed seeds. Look all you want, but there are no packets of Large Crabgrass or buckets of Carpetweed for the purchase. They just do not sell those kinds of seeds.

Mind blowing, I know.

But what would be even more mind blowing is if someone expected to find them for sale at these stores.

As a new homeowner myself, I have come to hate the sight of weeds in my flowerbed. In fact, I am convinced that all weeds are eternal—they never seem to die. I can spray and pull all I want, but nothing ever seems to stop them.

Like many living things, a weed's purpose is to grow and thrive. Although this is true, it is often at the expense of the actual plants around it. A weed's growth limits a garden's potential, not to mention the way that they taint its overall beauty.

Everyone knows that flowers are to grow in a garden, not weeds.

So you can imagine how shocking it would be for a Wal-Mart employee to have a customer who insists on buying themselves some weed seeds; it's just plain crazy. What kind of person would want weeds in their garden?

But in all honesty, we have a tendency to plant dozens of weeds in the gardens of our hearts each and every day.

A couple of chapters ago, we spoke of the overcoming power that we all have because of Jesus' work on the cross, and last chapter I gave five "looks of shame" with which each of us can identify.

I intentionally wrote each of those chapters to highlight our tendency and disposition to *feel shameful about having shame.* Think about it. As you read how you were blameless in Christ, how many negative thoughts fled through your mind, saying that you were anything but that?

And last chapter, were you struggling with taking on the identity of your look of shame? If so, you may have in your heart and mind that you *are* a "Prisoner of the Past," a "Constant Comparer," or whichever characteristic matched you best.

But just because I struggle with balancing responsibilities does not mean that all I am is a "Heavy Plater." Each of those characteristics is a way that our shame exposes itself, not more titles to define ourselves with.

But without us even recognizing it, we can both feel shame for having shame while also seeing ourselves as our struggles and sin. Every time we do this, it makes it harder and harder for us to self-forgive. Although this does not sound all that bad, what it is actually doing deep in our hearts is planting seeds of unforgiveness.

They are planted every time that we view ourselves without the grace of Christ; and if you are honest with yourself, we do that a lot. In the matter of a day, we view our bodies, our gifts, our situations, our personalities, our flaws, and our talents negatively. Each time we do this, we unknowingly plant seeds of unforgiveness in our own hearts.

When left untouched by God's grace, they have the potential to grow into a "root of bitterness," one that can truly disrupt both our lives and those closest to us.

The writer of Hebrews talks of this:

> See to it that no one fails to obtain the grace of God; that no root of bitterness springs up and causes trouble, and by it many become defiled.
>
> -Hebrews 12:15

Like weeds in a garden, these roots can grow and thrive, limiting the amount of attention that we can give to the fruit that we already do produce in our lives. Often, these "weeds" have become so *normal* to us, that we do not even consider them detrimental or harmful to our Christian walk.

But oh, they are.

And because who we are is so vast, so complex, these seeds of unforgiveness can be planted anywhere. Sometimes even deep inside of us, in places where we have not yet explored.

But where unforgiveness and bitterness is, grace is not.

I say all of this to highlight the truth that we *all* need to grace ourselves. Even if you do not recognize your own level of unforgiveness, please realize that those seeds are there. Each of us will always need to obtain more aspects of God's grace.

Or maybe you are dealing with the opposite; you are to the point of feeling completely overwhelmed with all of the "issues" that you currently have. Please read this: It is *normal* for us to have weeds in our garden.

We all have them and still choose to plant more.

You see, the process of overcoming unforgiveness is just another aspect of our spiritual journey. You would never expect a beginning driver to thrive in a six-lane highway, a toddler to know what food is the healthiest for them, or a newly married couple to know exactly what is best for each other.

This is because we know that each of these situations requires both time and practice. But please know that learning to grace ourselves while stopping the habit of planting unforgiveness is an over-time process as well.

It is evident in scripture that both Paul and Peter knew of the difficulty in recognizing and embracing God's grace. I believe that this is why they constantly charge their readers to seek the grace of God. If you do not believe me, look throughout their letters. You will find them continually bringing attention to the great need that we all have for grace.

In fact, Paul and Peter's main focus with grace is not for the reader to show grace to others, but for God's grace to "be with" them personally; for it to overwhelm each and every one of them.

They wanted their reader, and us now, to be fully graced by God.

So I challenge you to take this chapter seriously. In it, I will provide practical steps that we can all do on a daily basis to grace ourselves. I believe that with the help of the Holy Spirit, each of our weeds of unforgiveness can and will lessen, while God's rich grace abounds in and through us.

DAILY GRACE

When hearing the word grace, many different definitions may come to mind. They could range anywhere from Jesus giving us grace through the cross or to us being called to give grace and forgiveness to others in our life. Although this is true, it is not as common to view grace as something that we must also extend to ourselves.

In this perspective, it does not mean that we are giving ourselves our own grace, as if it is something from us. Instead, it means that we, as individuals, are stepping aside and letting Christ's grace overcome us every day. Even though grace is not from ourselves, we are the ones who choose to either withhold ourselves from it or allow ourselves to be embraced by it.

To put it simply, grace is the act of being given something that is completely undeserved. In the context of us extending grace to others, this definition is very easy to grasp.

When approaching poor and needy people, it seems rather natural for us to approach them with grace. Although we know that they do not "deserve" what we have, we know that it is right, and even righteous, for them to be fed or provided for.

To others, it seems much easier for us to react in grace by swiftly passing through the "undeserving" part. Although we know that the undeserving part is there, it only allows our grace to be more powerful to them.

But when gracing ourselves, we commonly react with two opposite extremes. We either let the "undeserving" part become a definite roadblock, or we choose for it to be something that we overlook and blot out.

The roadblock is created because deep in our hearts we know the unworthiness of our own thoughts. We know the perverted images that we replay in our minds. And we know how jealous and selfish we are.

The overlooking reaction comes when we decide to try and deceive ourselves by blocking out the reality of our sin. If we choose to not look too deep, our numbness allows us to easily show ourselves "grace," a cheap grace that is from us, not God.

But both of these reactions limit our ability to experience God's true grace in our own hearts. This is because when we choose to react in these ways, we miss the fact that grace is all about God's transformational power.

Before we go on, I would like for you to imagine a doll.

Yes, a doll.

But now, picture it worn, torn, and unsanitary. The dress on it, although pink and polka dotted, is also splattered with a mixture of mud, vomit, and urine. The hair is blonde, but the majority of it is missing, leaving the doll's head empty and ugly. Although a normal doll has all four limbs, this one is missing both a leg and an arm.

As you can tell, this doll is nasty and deserves the trash.

But right before your eyes you see a man pick it up, and with nothing but his own hands, he begins to work on it. As you sit in wonder, you see that this doll is being transformed. It suddenly has all four limbs, beautiful golden hair is starting to grow, and every blemish on the dress is washed clean.

If you would have shut your eyes during any point of this process or even just walked away because of the doll's grossness, your mind would have always pictured that doll as nasty. Even though it is now clean, your limited view would cause you to still consider it anything but.

Or, in a completely different case, if you choose to fool yourself into believing that the doll was never really that bad and began overlooking its problems, then the end transformation would seem less than glorious. Something "not that bad" became something good; what's the big deal?

But in reality, something old was made new. That doll was shown grace. And in order for us to see the true power and glory displayed, we have to recognize both the "before" and the "after."

Although it's a loose metaphor, the comparisons are strong.

In order for us to grace ourselves, two things must be done. One, we must acknowledge and bring into the light our sin and nastiness. And two, we must keep our eyes focused on all that God has done and is still doing with that sin and nastiness.

We may be slow to forgive ourselves, but God is the essence of forgiveness. He longs to show us more of it. Even though we once deserved to be thrown away with the trash, His Son showed us that His plans for us are much greater. Therefore, we must constantly have in mind that He is not yet finished.

And Paul writes about aspects of God's plan for us.

> The God of peace will soon crush Satan under your
> feet. The grace of our Lord Jesus Christ be with you.
> -Romans 16:20

Through grace, God plans to crush Satan. Specifically, Paul's words say that God plans on doing it under *our* feet—under OUR feet. When we acknowledge both our acts of sin and God's loving work through that sin, we are making way for this verse to happen. Through embracing grace, Satan will be crushed.

What an amazing promise!

Today's Grace

"Lord, give me the grace needed *today*—for both myself and for those around me." Without a doubt, this daily prayer has been the source of much transformation for me.

Hopefully by now you have learned that Satan works mainly in our "yesterdays" and in our "tomorrows." In fact, many of us, including myself, have unforgiveness that stems from past mistakes as well as future fears.

These past mistakes could be anything from missed opportunities, damaging failures, or harmful sins; while our future fears are us looking forward, imagining the worst, and choosing to not forgive ourselves for it now.

Although all of this sounds crazy, you know deep down that you do it often. This is why we constantly have restless and troubled spirits. But we must focus on the now. In therapy, this process is known as the "here-and-now."

So right now, this instant, focus on your "now."

Forget the argument that you had this morning, the interview that you have later today, the images that you looked at last night, and all of the "have-to's" on today's to-do list. Ask God to give you the grace needed right now. Yes, we do not deserve it; but without a doubt, we all need it.

The grace of God is given to us in the present, and then extended to our past and future. Let me reiterate that: the grace of God, the very thing that you need in order to go on in life, is given *right now*, and then it extends and overflows into your past and your future.

Although we do not like to admit it, our past will never change. We cannot hope for grace to change those actions from sin into obedience; that is not possible. But what we can do is focus on the grace of today, believing that it will change the *outcome* of our past.

The sin, the mistake, is going to always be sin. But grace given today can allow us to move past it. We must focus on now.

And with this focus on today, God's grace can produce in us a constant hope of the future, not an irrational fear of the worst. Living in His present grace, we can clearly see and experience His blessings as they come. They are there, crammed within our worries and fears. What we must do, however, is slow down and ask Him to give us the clarity needed to recognize them.

God's word tells us that His grace is sufficient, that it is exactly what we need and exactly enough for us. We feel restless, troubled, shameful, and chaotic because we are missing that His grace is exactly what we need.

As you continue on, let this be the prayer of your day: "God give me the grace that I need right now; let me know that it is enough."

I'm Okay with My Clay

So at this point, your thoughts may sound a little like this:

> This all seems way too simple. I need to just "pray for
> grace right now," and then I will *magically* feel better?
> I doubt it. God doesn't work like that.

And honestly, I do not blame you for those thoughts.

It is extremely hard to believe that God's grace can actually make things better. It is difficult to see our sins through His eyes and even more difficult to see ourselves through it.

With that said, I have decided to give two more simple applications to help us find daily grace.

The first being this: "I am okay with my clay because God is here."

There are days when my spirit gets overly troubled. These are the days that I seem too easily irritated and way too eager to be done with everything. My failures seem to pile up and my expectations of myself are unmet. It is during these times that I am unable to see God's grace around me and in me.

So I get alone, sit down, and call to the forefront of my mind that "I am okay in my clay because God is here." This short and simple statement, when said truthfully, provides me with an avenue back to God's grace.

Although this seems easy enough, it actually implies a couple of harder things. One, it calls me to do what we learned before by focusing on myself *right now*; for it is where grace is. And two, it calls me to *separate myself* from right now.

Yes, you read that correctly. Grace is found when we focus on both the present while also separating ourselves from it.

If you think about it, when we are troubled, shameful, and constantly unforgiving of ourselves, our present situation does not seem to help us change those feelings.

In fact, your "right now" may consist of you having to live in the consequences of your past sins. Your "right now" may seem to be a time of hardship after hardship. Or your "right now" may be full of people and things that show you everything but grace.

This is why that statement is so needed.

At your core, the fact is that you are okay. But in order for us to see that, many times we must separate ourselves from where we are and what seems to be all around us. Even though you may be living in the consequences of your sin, His grace is still found in you; and you in Him.

In fact, scripture says that we are and will *always* be found in Jesus. So even though we may "find" ourselves acting in sin or living in times of hardship, we must remember that at our core, we are found in Him; in His grace. Although we are jars of clay, we are more.

Our current situations may provide an avenue toward unforgiveness, but remembering our real security in Jesus provides an avenue toward grace.

Last night, last week, or even last year, you may have done things that you are now regretting. Instead of planting unforgiveness in your heart, seek God's grace and realize that deep down, you are okay because He is in you.

Although we disobey and sin, we are no longer defined by that sin. In fact, our lives are under a law of grace, a law of freedom. These are Paul's words written to the Church in Rome:

> What then? Shall we sin because we are not under law
> but under grace? By no means!
>
> -Romans 6:15

> Now that you have been set free from sin and have
> become slaves to God, the benefit you reap leads to
> holiness, and the result is eternal life.
>
> -Romans 6:22

You see, our "okayness" is only because God's grace has allowed us to reap holiness and eternal life. So even though you may currently be in a place of chaos and hardship, God's promise proclaims that it will not always remain.

My challenge, then, is for you to put into practice the principle of separating yourself from your current situation and remembering that you are okay. Because of God's work in you, your life is geared toward holiness and eternal peace.

Where we are now is not where we will always be.

Bring Your Weeds into the Light

But for some of you, focusing on the now seems too difficult, praying for God to help seems too inadequate, and separating yourself from your present seems too impossible.

What you may need, then, is to bring your weeds into the light; to actively dispose of them. Scripture says that this is done through confession; and that being to others, not just to God.

Maybe what you need is to tell someone what you have done, tell someone what you are feeling, tell someone the thoughts that you are having, or tell someone the situation that you are finding yourself in.

If this sounds intimidating, then write it out, hand it to a friend, and discuss it later. The fact is that weeds of unforgiveness will continually abound if grace is never shown or experienced.

Although the Catholic tradition receives much criticism for how they handle confession, I believe that they grasp the deeper meaning attached to this discipline in ways that we in the Evangelical tradition do not. One Catholic author wrote this:

> "It is in the act of expressing sorrow for my sin that the grace of contrition began to flow into me.... Something happens in the discipline as you hear yourself articulate your own shame. The penitent becomes more real by another human being's acceptance in the light of truth."

In my own experience, confession has always provided me with a beautiful example of what grace looks like. Although we will uncover this more in an upcoming chapter, there is one point that I must express now.

When I first decided to tell people my weeds, I was shocked by how easily they looked through them and saw *me*. Every time that I disclosed my deepest places of unforgiveness, I was met with an abundance of grace.

Each person's ability to love me despite my situation, my struggles, or my past showed me more and more aspects of God's forgiveness. More than anything else, their grace toward me taught me how to grace myself.

As the quote above states, repentance becomes more real to our hearts when we experience the grace-filled acceptance from others.

And this is the reason why I challenge you to confess your unforgiveness to someone. Without a doubt, I know that you will be completely surprised by the amount of grace that God's people can muster up for you. This is because when you confess and make known all of your scars, cracks, and dents—those broken parts of you that have filled you with shame—your hearers experience God.

When we make known our sins, people see God shining through them. Being broken vessels, our confessed cracks only allow our inner treasure to be seen more vividly. That is the power of the gospel: that Jesus takes our past sins and shines his grace through them.

So bring your weeds into the light.

Although you can compile a number of reasons and excuses to not do it, the fact is that it may be the most powerful way for you to learn grace. So find someone you trust, practice the discipline of confession, and experience God's unending forgiveness.

Active Grace

Although I have touched on three simple ways to practically grace ourselves, know that it does not end here. God's grace is greater than I could ever hope to explain.

With that said, I challenge you to seek God's word for more of what His grace means to us. You and I are very needy people, but God says that He meets all of those needs through the grace that He extends to us. So search the truths found in scripture for what that means. Below, I have included some great starting points, but do not let the search end there.

Grace is:

    From God's FULLNESS…John 1:16

    Through Jesus…John 1:17

And it:

    Gives us great power to speak up…Acts 4:33; Ephesians 3:8

    Gives us power to do great wonders and signs…Acts 6:8

    Gives us Salvation…Acts 15:11; Ephesians 2:8

    Builds us up and gives us Christ's inheritance…Acts 20:32

    Allows us to bring others to obedience and faith…Romans 1:5

    Is an undeserved gift…Romans 3:24

    Allows us to stand and rejoice with hope…Romans 5:2

    Gives us gifts to use for Christ…Romans 12:6

    Gives boldness and power over Satan…Romans 15:15; 16:20

    Gives us purpose…1 Corinthians 3:10

    Makes us who we are meant to be…1 Corinthians 15: 10

    Allows us to abound in good works…2 Corinthians 9:8

    Is sufficient for our every need…2 Corinthians 12:9

    It calls us to be more than we are…Galatians 1:6; 15

    Forgives us daily…Ephesians 1:7

    Is given to us for others…Ephesians 3:2

    Overflows us with Christ's faith and love…1 Timothy 1:14

    Gives us strength when we are weak…2 Timothy 2:1

    Gives us confidence to approach Christ…Hebrews 4:16

    It restores, confirms, and establishes us…1 Peter 5:10

QUESTIONS FOR REFLECTION

1. What are some of your own weeds of unforgiveness?

2. In the context of gracing yourself, which extreme do you normally fall into:
   Do you tend to let your "undeservedness" be a roadblock for grace OR Do you have the tendency to overlook and lessen your sin with cheap grace?

3. Out of the three practical steps addressed earlier (*Today's Grace, I'm Okay, and Bringing Your Weeds into Light*), which one(s) stood out to you the most? Why?

4. After reading through some of the previous verses, is there anything new about God's grace that you learned?

5. Read 1 Corinthians 1:4-9.
   What is Paul saying about God's grace here?

CHAPTER 12

PURSUING
POSITIVE PLEASURES

*"God whispers to us in our pleasures
[and] speaks to us in our conscience...."*
-C.S. Lewis

If someone were to create a list titled "The 20 Most Shameful Moments in scripture," I am pretty sure that the foretold story of Peter denying the already betrayed Jesus would make top five; hands-down.

> I tell you the truth, before the rooster crows, you will disown me three times!
>
> - John 13:38

Amazed that Jesus would say this, Peter quickly defends his adoration for his Lord. However, to no one's surprise, in just a few short hours Peter denies every bit of his love and affiliation with Jesus to a slave-girl, a group of people around a charcoal fire, and lastly, to the slave of a high priest.

Even after being warned, Peter chooses to spit in the face of his Lord. Worry, fear, and anxieties led him to deny every bit of association with Jesus, the author of peace.

And just as Jesus predicted, after the third denial, a rooster crowed. In every one of the Gospels, the story ends the scene here, with the imagery of Peter hearing the crow and realizing what he had just done…three times.

Although it does not inexplicably say this, there is no doubt in my mind that Satan proudly used the crow of that rooster to bring about a depth and heaviness of shame inside of Peter:

> *Peter, all of the progress that you have made and every ounce of the relationship that you had with Jesus…are all gone. You are nothing but a hypocrite; a failure.*

In the Gospel of John, this epic denial is the last time that we hear of Peter until after Jesus is resurrected. Although we have no way of knowing the extent of Peter's shame during Jesus' trial and crucifixion, we do know that God was not yet done with him. In fact, Chapter 21 of John depicts the resurrected Jesus approaching Peter in an environment that was very dear to Peter's heart.

John writes that one night, while seven of the disciples were together, Peter decided that he would go fishing (21:3).

In scripture, this statement appears quite randomly, but in reality, this was not out of character for Peter. We learn early on in the gospels that Peter was a well-known fisherman; one who truly loved the sea. And the heart of every fisherman finds true *pleasure* in the catch.

Although going out to fish was originally Peter's decision, John writes that the other six chose to accompany him to Tiberias. For hours, the seven of them eagerly casted out their nets in anticipation. To their dismay, however, they caught absolutely nothing.

As dawn approaches, we read that Jesus appeared, standing on the shoreline. Although the seven did not recognize Him at first, they soon realized that they were once again in the presence of their Lord.

Instantly, Peter puts on an outer robe, jumps into the water, and swims toward his Savior. The rest of the story is a crazy mixture of awkwardly convicting questions, vulnerable answers, and a beautiful reconciliation at the end.

In this chapter, Jesus meets Peter at his place of pleasure.

THE POWER OF PLEASURE

Before you freak out with my use of the word "pleasure," I am going to ask you to do something powerful: from now on, separate the word pleasure from the tainting work of sin. Yes, in this chapter, I will never team up the word "pleasure" with any form of lust, selfish pursuit, or sinful desire.

In its truest form, pleasure is nothing but a gift that God graces upon us as His children. In its truest form, pleasure is good. And I believe wholeheartedly that the pursuit of these true pleasures can help each of us vanquish the effects of shame in our lives.

I am not saying that pursuing pleasures are a direct formula to becoming shame-free, but instead, that they are a powerful tool that can lead both you and me to a place where we can be met by Jesus Christ; for He is the only real "formula" toward becoming shame-free.

Even though I have witnessed Jesus' power through the pursuit of positive pleasures, it is not a concept that I came up with on my own. In fact, C.S. Lewis is one of the first to write about this idea in his book, *The Screwtape Letters*.

He writes that true pleasures are "the deepest likings and impulses of any man." It is these impulses that make up the "raw material" that God chooses to work with when He transforms us into new creations.

You see, when God handmade each of us, He gave us an identity that was different than anyone else's. In fact, the personality that you have, the gifts that you work with, the talents that you use, and the mind that you think with are all vastly different than even my own. And each of us contains "likings" and "impulses" that make us...us.

As the Spirit works toward transforming our lives, He does not discount or overlook our individual selves. Instead, God uses those deep likings and pleasures to both meet us where we are and to bring us more into the people that we are called to be.

When making us more like Himself, Jesus calls us forward and highlights the very things that make us different. In fact, we are most like Christ when we act and behave most like ourselves. That sounds strange, but it is true. When you put aside facades, take off masks, and live as *yourself*—a new creation with special qualities, gifts, and abilities—you shine Christ more vividly.

Peter's personality—his deep liking—was for the sea. Although Bible scholars are in disagreement with whether or not this trip to Tiberias was done in disobedience, my personal opinion is that Peter was not "sinning" by the *act* of fishing. It was something that his heart *enjoyed*. Matthew Henry, a theologian and commentator, writes this:

> "It was rather commendable in them [the disciples];
> for they did it to redeem time, and not be idle. They
> were not yet appointed to preach the resurrection of
> Christ. Their commission was in the drawing, but
> not perfected. The hour for entering upon action was

to come... Now, in the meantime, rather than do nothing, they would go fishing."

Although Jesus did tell them to be filled with the Holy Spirit in John 20, the designated time for this to happen would be later in Acts. Because of this, they had no command or commission to do otherwise. Therefore, Peter went back to his old occupation. He returned to a place of pleasure. And what we find in the story is that it was Peter who recognized Jesus on the shore.

In some weird way, fishing provided Peter with the opportunity to step back and realize reality. To him, fishing felt comfortable, peaceful, and homey. C.S. Lewis states that our pleasures are "unmistakably real, and therefore, give the man who feels them a touchstone of reality."

When experiencing positive pleasures, we become attune with pieces of reality. We forget fears and shame and simply *be*. The starry sky and beautiful sounds of the waves knocking against his boat created a perfect environment for Peter to step away from his shame. He was present, enjoying life and exercising his gifts.

And just like Peter, it is when we simply "be" that we are met, in reality, by Jesus.

If you are familiar with this passage, then you know that the story does not just end after Peter reaches the shore. In fact, John writes that Jesus sat at a fire, ate breakfast, and had an intentional conversation with Peter. And three times, Jesus asks Peter those awkwardly convicting questions:

> When they had finished breakfast, Jesus said to Simon
> Peter, "Simon son of John, do you love Me more than
> these?" He said to Him, "Yes, Lord; You know that

I love You." Jesus said to him, "Feed My lambs." A
second time He said to him, "Simon son of John, do
you love Me?" He said to Him, "Yes, Lord; You know
that I love You." Jesus said to him, "Tend My sheep."
He said to him the third time, "Simon son of John,
do you love Me?" Peter felt hurt because He said to
him the third time, "Do you love Me?" And he said
to Him, "Lord, You know everything; You know that
I love You." Jesus said to him, "Feed My sheep."

-John 21:15-17

Although Jesus could have left Peter on the Sea of Tiberias, He
chose to bring him in close and give him a glimpse of his calling. Of
course, the elephant in the room had to be dealt with (Peter's triple
denial), but afterwards, Jesus goes straight into His glorious plan
for Peter.

It was there on the shoreline that Jesus showed Peter grace, called
him to reclaim his love, and reminded him of his role in the Kingdom
of God. Peter was called to be a shepherd; to feed and tend God's
flock. This Apostle's personal commission was given to him at his
place of pleasure.

This is profound.

Just as C.S. Lewis wrote, Peter's "likings" and his "impulses" were
a foundation that God used to mold him into the man that he was
designed to become. For now on, he would not be catching fish to eat,
sell, and provide for himself with. Instead, he would be taking on the
role of a shepherd, "feeding" and providing for others.

The Enemy and Pleasure
Satan hates true pleasures.

He knows that they are blessings in life that point toward God. Positive pleasures work against his schemes. In fact, in *The Screwtape Letters*, Lewis words it this way (keep in mind that his whole book is written from the perspective of a demon writing letters to a "younger" demon):

> "How can you have failed to see that a *real* pleasure was the last thing you ought to have let him meet?... That it would peel off from his sensibility the kind of crust you have been forming on it, and make him feel that he was coming home, recovering himself?"

In this letter, Lewis highlights that our *real* pleasures can "de-crust" the hardness that the enemy so hopes to produce in our hearts. While shame is being formed, Satan tries to thicken it through continual acts of idle sin and accusation. If he can keep us from true pleasures, he can keep us numb and passive.

Lewis carries it further:

> "The man who truly and disinterestedly enjoys any one thing in the world, for its own sake, and without caring two-pence what other people say about it, is by that very fact forearmed against some of our subtlest modes of attack."

Our en*joyment*, true *joy*-filled enjoyment, is from God. When it is done apart from unrighteous fear or sin, these pleasures *forearm* us against the hidden attacks of Satan. True pleasures help us in our spiritual lives!

So in an attempt to postpone or even destroy our journey out of shame, Satan will do one of two things: distort our pleasures or limit our ability to experience them.

A distorted pleasure breaks down the innocence of the original act and mixes in selfishness, pride, insecurities, false motives, deceit, anger, or bitterness.

It is the moment when exercise is no longer about remaining healthy, but instead a constant pursuit of "looking sexier," being "better," getting "more respect," or being more "manly." It is when spending time with friends becomes merely an opportunity to gossip about others and bash all of those who are "less than" you. And it is when doing that assignment, playing that sport, or finishing that project is more about pleasing a parent, showing off your success, or proving that you are good enough.

When tainted, pleasures can become major factors in our cycle of shame. For instance, deep down, you may long for connection. But in your shame, you do not feel like you deserve it. So you find yourself pursuing sexual pleasures to gain approval and to feel "loved."

And this does not only mean with other people. One of the most addicting forms of distorted pleasure is through pornography. Your positive pleasure of connection is tainted, only providing you with more longing and desire. But because you know it is wrong, Satan feeds you shame. And the cycle continues.

All of this is the work of Satan. If he can make us falsely pursue pleasures, then he can keep us away from ever experiencing reality. That reality is this: Jesus desires to meet us where we are, exactly how we are.

The same is true for those times when the enemy aims at limiting or entirely taking away our positive pleasures. Lewis writes:

"The great thing is to prevent his doing anything...
Let him do anything but act. No amount of piety
in his imagination and affections will harm us if we
can keep it out of his will...The more often he feels
without acting, the less he will be able to ever act, and,
in the long run, the less he will be able to feel."

This is the spiral effect of a pleasureless life. We all know these times. They are the moments when our days are too hectic and too long to squeeze in any actual enjoyment. Our busy schedules end up providing Satan with powerful means of distracting us from pursuing pleasures. We get home, lie on the couch, eat dinner, and sleep.

We think about acting and perhaps feel the need to act, but nothing is produced from those thoughts. Our wills remain passive, making our hearts susceptible for more shame and lies. We know all too well that guilty feeling of not doing what we deep down want and need to do.

"I just do not have the time or energy for that anymore."

And slowly, our lives become more and more normal. As we continually deny those feelings and impulses, we find that weeks will pass without us even thinking about slowing down.

The extraordinary that is all around us cannot be seen because we deny ourselves any opportunity to simply "be." We become like dormant volcanoes; there, but unaware of both our destined potential and our true identity.

In our fixation with busy schedules, we grow numb to the fact that Jesus longs to work in us and through us. He longs to use our pleasures.

Pleasuring Away Shame

Before I continue, I must repeat that this chapter is not a "do it yourself" chapter. For shame can only be taken away through the grace of God. So in order for "positive pleasures" to be just that, they must be done in faith. They must be acted upon with innocence and humility, apart from sin.

It is the moments of realizing and pursuing these things that we no longer find the need to feel shameful. Positive pleasures always allow us to gain more glimpses of God and His reason for making us. In fact, we discover more of ourselves through pursuing these impulses.

C.S. Lewis himself met God through pursing his positive pleasure. If you study his biography you learn that, originally, he had no desire to follow a "god." His love was for literature. He had such a passion for reading eloquent writings that it consumed much of his time.

Soon, this exact love would lead him to the Author of Life. The more that he pursued this passion, the more that he could not see life without a God. In fact, it was through the pleasure and enjoyment of reading that C.S. Lewis found Jesus. And as we know, God used his pleasure to bring out his calling.

Your Pleasures

So now it is time for you to answer. What are your impulses and likings? What are the things that you have a strong bent toward pursuing?

For me, it is running.

And all of those close to me know this, especially my wife. When I get stressed, uneasy, and even unconfident about my life, Kate tells me to go outside and run. This is because for years, God has used running as my time of being.

It is the time when I can get away from my life and simply be myself; be Greg. Without a doubt, God has spoken to me more often while I was on a run than any other time. I can honestly look back and see so many life-changing realizations that took place while on foot.

This is because the Lord meets me when I am most *me*.

Again I ask you, what are your pleasures? Not your selfish and impure urges, but the positive core likings that are within you.

For some of you it may pertain to getting alone and reading a good book, blogging, journaling, walking on a secluded trail, watching a good movie, fishing at a private place, hunting early in the morning, retreating to a nearby campsite, going on a run or jog, watching a sunset or sunrise, or going out to the nearest mountain range to climb and boulder.

And for others of you, your pleasures may also include people. Perhaps yours is going out to eat with a friend, working out with a buddy, going out to a nearby coffee shop, spending a day shopping with a sister, or perhaps inviting friends over to your own home.

Yes, these are simple pleasures. But please do not discount the power in pursuing your heart's deepest likings. God has created you with those longings.

Personally, I feel free and clear of mind when I go running, something that is definitely needed after becoming a new father to a pair of twins. In fact, if I did not get out and alone, my days would squeeze together and become ordinary and mundane. I would forget the passion and drive that God chose to create within me; a passion that I believe the enemy is truly afraid of. This is because God uses running to constantly solidify my identity in Him.

Your pleasures, whatever they may be, are powerful avenues out of shame and toward Jesus Christ. They are a great tool for self-discovery because they are a great tool for discovering God.

Please search for your own. Then truly ask yourself if you are willing to take time out of your busy schedule and confidently pursue them.

Maybe you should start today. Or now.

QUESTIONS FOR REFLECTION

1. What are your thoughts/feelings toward the idea of us pursuing pleasures in order to fight shame?

2. What do you believe are some of your positive pleasures?

3. In what ways has God met you at these "impulses" and "likings" before?

4. Is the idea of *"being"* worth the time it takes to pursue it?

CHAPTER 13

THE CALL
FOR COMMUNION

"I live in the faith that there is a Presence and Power greater
than I am that nurtures and supports me in ways I could not
even imagine. I know that this Presence is All-Knowing and
All-Powerful and is always right where I am...."
-Ernest Holmes

I have come to realize that we, as *lovers* of Christ, have a small and narrow view of intimacy with Him.

Yes, *intimacy.*

I say this because of our strong fascination with those rare "God" moments in life. Those powerful worship services, intense conversations, or precious times of prayer that seem to provide us with a "mountain top experience."

Although there is nothing wrong with these moments, the problem exists in the amount of emphasis that we place on them. Without even realizing it, we can elevate them to the point of regarding them *as* our relationship with Christ, as if they provide us with a way to gage our "level of intimacy."

Think about it, how often do you view your closeness with God in terms of your last great experience?

"Well, last month at camp I grew so much…so God and I are super close right now."

OR…

"I attend church every week, but I just haven't *felt it* during worship like I did that one night…I must be far from God."

Although these are simple examples, they do not negate how true this is.

We tend to base our relationship with God on the "feelings" of intimacy that our last grand experience gave us.

As the gap between these experiences becomes larger and larger, our hearts begin to believe that God is distant; like our current relationship with Him is nowhere close to where it once was. In this distance, God may feel silent.

The feeling that this produces is well known by each of us. This is because in our shame, we feel *far* from God.

But know, once again, that this feeling is based off of a small and narrow view of intimacy. Even though we need those mountain top experiences, they are, in no way, the full extent of intimacy that God desires to have with us. In fact, God longs for and calls for us to have true *communion* with Him daily.

Now, when I say the word "communion," I am not speaking of the little cracker and 2 ounce cup of juice that we get in worship services. Communion is defined by the overall connection that we have with God; the life-long, always-happening, connection.

It is more than taking the Lord's Supper, reading His Word five times a week, and praying before bed. What God desires is for us to recognize and respond to His constant presence around us and in us *every day*. He wants a relationship that extends past those great experiences.

You see, if we believe that the presence of the Lord is with us always, then we must also believe that the Spirit of the Lord is always at work in us, even when we feel far from Him. For where God is, God works.

In fact, the truest form of intimacy is discovered *on the journey to* those grand experiences. It is found in the difficult and strenuous valleys between the mountains; those times of bitterness, dullness, and numbness. And even though every feeling in us is shouting that we are far from God, what we need is to realize that God is surrounding us at all times.

Those feelings, although powerful, are foundationless; they hold no truth.

Yes, we may miss out on the intimacy that God is calling us to have with Him, but He is not distant. As Robert Mulholland depicts, there is actually a lot going on underneath the surface of our foundationless feelings:

> "What we don't realize is that often a period of apparent spiritual stagnation, a time in which we don't feel as if we are going anywhere, a phase of life in which our relationship with God seems weak or nonexistent, the time of dryness, of darkness—is actually filled with nurturing down below the surface that we never see…And what we see as a quantum leap forward may actually be only the smallest part of what has been going on in a long, steady process of grace…."

Although we see our growth as pivotal moments, God desires us to be enlightened toward seeing and feeling the continual growth that is always there. When the valleys point to anything but closeness to God, what is actually happening is a powerful ripening of our faith. Through our struggle, He is working, pruning, transforming, shaping.

Can you imagine what it would be like to put our feelings aside and constantly acknowledge that growth?

Our relationship with God would become so rich.

We would not only look at great lengths with Him on the mountaintops, but also walk alongside of Him through the dry and weariness of the valleys. But communion like this does not come naturally. It is something that must be learned and practiced often.

But practically, how do we do this?

What does this look like to answer God's call for communion?

AWKWARD, BUT TRUE FELLOWSHIP

First off, communion is awkward.

I write this because of my current situation. Although I am sitting alone at a coffee shop, I cannot help but overhear the conversation of a young dating couple sitting within feet of me.

I am normally not a creeper like this, I promise, but right now I am so intrigued by them. Here is just a small example of what is going on next to me:

> "What did you do this weekend?"
> (response)
> "Oh wow! I bet you had a blast. Were you tired afterward?"

(response)

"Hahaha…I can imagine…."

(…pause…)

The awkwardness of their small talk has my own stomach churning. On their faces, I see excitement and eagerness—with a hint of uncertainty. Each one of them is leaning into the table talk. This must be a new relationship.

Oh, I remember this stage all too well.

When first dating anyone, it is always the same. You want to know and learn all about the other person, while seeking to also reveal aspects of who you are to them. Your eyes and ears are focused. And the awkward part is the newness of it all.

But as I sit here, I cannot help but compare this to our own communion with God.

Here are two beings, longing to get to know each other better. It is early on Monday morning, so these two have intentionally made time for this. And together, they eagerly communicate, regardless of how simple the conversation may initially be.

In fact, something truly complex is happening under the surface of their simple conversation. Every word said and heard allows another string to be tied in their relationship.

She wants to know how his weekend went and he wants to know of the concerns that she has regarding some of her friends. With every disclosed answer, they work toward building up and strengthening their bond.

Without a doubt, this is what God desires.

He wants us to long to know Him more; to eagerly listen for what He has to say. And He wants us to let Him in on our own lives and concerns; He wants a *united* relationship.

But how often are we that intentional? How often do we wake up early on Monday morning for coffee with God? How often do we ask God questions to answer? And how often do we eagerly listen to all that He has to say to us?

> "God, what did you do this weekend in my life/in the
> world around me?
> (response)
> "God, where are you at work today?"
> (response)

I am convinced that God is so ready and willing to answer these questions. But are we ready and willing to ask…and to listen? Perhaps our unwillingness is because we have a hard time expecting that He will actually respond to us. And if He does respond, how can we hear it? What if we get it wrong? What if we do the wrong thing? Or what if He tells us something that we do not want to hear?

The list of concerns can go on and on.

But these thoughts are what make a relationship a *real relationship*. It is the awkwardness of it all that proves that it is true. Although I cannot hear the thoughts of the couple sitting close to me, I am fairly confident that both are questioning every word that flows from their own mouths.

This is because both of them are uncertain about this new relationship. But before every "date," they each have to decide whether or not the experience of getting to know each other is better than living in the fear of those uncertainties.

Yet as I sit here now, I can vividly see what option they each have chosen.

But now let's talk about you.

Yes, you can think of a dozen reasons why you should not try and commune with God. But scripture says that those who seek Him will find Him. And in order for communion to happen, you and I have to decide to deny those foundationless feelings of uncertainty and choose to seek His voice. Dallas Willard said it this way:

> "When I seek for something, I look for it everywhere. It's when we *seek* God earnestly, prepared to go out of our way to examine anything that might be His overture toward us—including obvious things like Bible verses or our own thoughts—that He promises to be found (Jeremiah 29:13). But we'll be able to seek Him only if we honestly believe that He might explicitly address us in ways suitable to His purposes in our lives."

God will speak to us, for we are His. And there is a strong aspect of communion that calls us to get up out of the pit of our shameful feelings and actually seek to grow with Him.

However, this growth is gradual. Because of that, I have decided to provide you with three practical disciplines that have proven, in my own life, to be great pathways toward communion.

They are simple, yet complex. Through discipline and perseverance, true and consistent conversation with God can take place. Because they are steps toward relational growth, they will probably feel awkward at times. But I challenge you to try them out.

The shame of being far from God will only end once we become aware of and truly experience His constant presence.

The Recurring Voice in Us

One of the most common paths for hearing God's words is through the thoughts of our own spirit. But even as you read that, many of you may disregard it as a fact. But the truth, as Paul states, is that "we have the mind of Christ" (1 Corinthians 2:16).

It is through our hearts and minds that the Lord both discloses more of himself and redeems the entirety of who we are. This, however, seems to be quite contrary to what we have been taught for years: that our thoughts should not be trusted for they are desperately wicked and inherently bad.

But to fully take on a view like this can actually harm our understanding of and ability to hear God speak. Don't get me wrong; there is an important distinction between God's thoughts and the thoughts of a person who is without God.

But in Christ, we are graced with the ability to think with Him; to think *His thoughts*. Dallas Willard says this:

> "We must not obscure the simple fact that God comes to us precisely in and through our thoughts, perceptions, and experiences, and that He can approach our conscious life *only* through them, for they are the substance of our lives…God's gracious incursions into our souls can make our thoughts His thoughts."

This concept is so important to our growth and development with Christ. If God speaks to us through our own ideas, thoughts, and feelings, are we aware of what comes to our mind that could be of Him?

I believe that many of us have God's very Spirit whispering in our minds more often than we may think. Although this true, we tend to regard them as anything *but* His Spirit's words.

Think about it.

How many times do you feel like you should do something, but then question it long enough to discover that the opportunity is no longer there? And then we just make the conclusion that it "must've not been what God wanted."

Many times, these thoughts are ones that are recurring.

For instance, the past few months, you may have had an idea centered on a certain people group; one that has had you thinking about them quite often. Although this is true, you may have continually denied its importance—or maybe you have even disregarded that you were the one to step up and do something with those thoughts.

Or perhaps you constantly pass that same kid every day, and for some reason your mind focuses on him/her for the next five minutes. But because you are so unaware of the power in this, you disregard the thought and continue on in your day.

But these situations are the voice of God in us; the soft inkling that urges us to stop that, to start this, to go there, to slow down here, or to speak over there. This is the Holy Spirit *speaking to* and *guiding* us.

When God is in someone, His Spirit's work is spread throughout their whole selves. And as we grow in Him, we begin to realize that He invades and reshapes our very thoughts.

But many times, we are unaware of this and continue to live our lives as if He does not speak to us. Our shame has us focused on anything but the good that God has planned for us to do. The result is that those recurring thoughts are left on the back burner of our minds, never touched or dealt with.

But I challenge you, when thoughts become recurring, stop and prayerfully consider what they mean. If they continue to happen and are not blatantly against scripture…then do them. For I am convinced that Satan's work is to keep us questioning them just long enough for us to miss the opportunity that they posed.

And in all honesty, why would Satan soften your heart toward a certain people group? Or point you in a direction of a person who is in need of Christ? He wouldn't.

Because we are hidden in Jesus, we must open up our consciousness to the fact that He has a longing to speak to us and *through* us.

So listen for that recurring voice.

The Voice of Scripture

Scripture is powerful; it is the very *word* of God; His own message to the world. But do you realize that every time you read it, you are literally engaging with the words that He has spoken long ago; words that are still being spoken by Him today?

I ask this because there is an aspect of our hearts that still has a hard time believing in the power of God's Word. In fact, many times we approach scripture as a formula to answer our questions. We want it to give us the feelings that we want and we search it for some special knowledge.

In doing this, we soon find ourselves at a place where passages begin to feel dry, repetitive, and pointless. But the power of scripture is not found solely in the written words themselves, but in the Spirit of God who is *still* speaking the words to us, His followers.

As I said at the start of this chapter, we tend to have a small and narrow view of our intimacy with God. This is why we approach scripture as a book that we simply *read*, whether alone or in a church body.

Reading implies that *we* are the ones in control. *We* pick up the word of God, read it as *we* see fit, decide what *we* want to learn, and put it down when *we* are finished—or bored. It becomes a means toward a "fix" or a check off of our to-do list instead of being inspired words that are both spoken and alive.

The power of the Bible—what separates it from any other published work—is that it is *beyond readable*. Anyone can open up its pages, soak in the words, and gain both insight and application from a passage. But without the Spirit's voice, without His help, the Word of God will not be understood.

Scripture is beyond readable because true insight and overall transformation come solely by the Spirit working in us. It is He who awakens our hearts, minds, and souls to the depth of His divine knowledge. Without His voice, the Word of God cannot be internalized.

This is because God's word is not a "thing" to read, but an intimate voice to hear. If we are going to have a relationship with Him, we must lose our control in reading and choose to discipline ourselves to simply listen.

A strong relationship requires listening. And the couple that sat before me understood that. Yes, they prompted questions for each other, but they, in no way, controlled the response. Why? Because they genuinely wanted to hear from the other.

And communion with God starts from an initial want and grows into hearing His Spirit speak the words that He has spoken for eternity.

But what does this actually look like?

For years, believers have taken part in an age-old discipline known as "*lectio divina.*" In short, this is a tool used to focus our hearts on hearing, with the understanding that God *is* there. Through this discipline, the doer engages every aspect of themselves—their senses, reason, imagination, memory, emotions, and will—to God.

With that said, this overall exercise has four main parts to it: reading, meditation, prayer, and contemplation.

When I first began this practice, I was not aware of its true level of difficulty. Even though I say this, I was also not aware of how transformational it would be when put into practice.

The first part is as simple as it sounds; you find a passage and you read it. Please keep in mind that *longer* does not mean better. Open to a few verses and read them over and over until your mind has a strong familiarity with the written words.

Then comes meditation. This part of the exercise requires nothing but you, the Spirit, and time. To be completely honest, this is one of the most difficult steps for us Americans. We live in a culture that tells us to do anything but slow down.

But for true communion to happen, we must choose to sit with the words we read and open up our hearts to hear them come alive. During this time of meditation, aspects of the verses may come to your mind. Dwell on them. Question them. And dwell more.

This is the third part of *lectio divina*: prayer. When the word is meditated upon, the Spirit invades our minds. Because His thoughts are becoming our thoughts, what comes to our minds *is* Him speaking. Our prayers then are for clarity, for answers to why *that* specific verse or word came to mind. Why *that* phrase brought up *those* emotions in you. And why *that* random thought is still invading your mind.

And as we pray, we continually meditate and pray more.

Then, through much discipline, we may find ourselves at the point of contemplation. I say "through much discipline" because many of our times of *lectio divina* will never make it to this final step. This is because contemplation requires a peaceful and contrite heart.

It is the point where we simply relax and soak up God's presence. Unlike our worry-filled days, contemplation brings us to a place of complete "okay-ness," much like I spoke about in chapter 11.

Here, we are content with awaiting His words. The perfect image of this is a married couple that has spent a whole evening strengthening their relationship and has now found themselves at a place with nothing more to say to each other. In the stillness, they look intently in each other's eyes, being completely content with the silence.

It is here that God may give us a specific task, word, or purpose. But this is not always so, for contemplation is merely us having a posture of submission. Even though *lectio divina* is finished after this stage, it is designed to always be happening; to constantly challenge us to revisit those questions and concerns.

For many believers, the practice of these four steps has truly transformed lives and levels of intimacy with God. And this is what I hope for you as well. *Lectio Divina* is not *the* answer to your feeling of dryness and shame, Jesus is. But it does allow us to re-center our hearts and minds on His presence.

With that said, I urge you to begin this discipline.

It may feel too structured, but the truth is that a shameful heart posture tends to be one of chaos. This is why we have a hard time deciphering God's voice amidst our day. With that said, structure may be exactly what you have needed for a long time. So practice it and build some spiritual discipline.

The Voice of Prayer

Although the discipline of prayer is included in *lectio divina*, it should not be limited to that practice only. For when we speak to God, we are talking, in the real world, to a Being who created this real world.

And lives are changed through prayer.

However, what I have discovered and even have been convicted of is how easy it is to *ramble* and how hard it is to *pray*. In fact, I have an uncanny ability in thinking about thoughts that could be prayers, but never allowing them to actually address God.

I can think good thoughts all day, seek to muster up the feeling of happiness, think about my need to get over my insecurities, or even think about how beautiful it is outside, but in all cases, I never allow them to address God through prayer.

What God wants is for us to include Him in all of our thoughts. Instead of just trying to build up the feelings of confidence, He desires us to actually ask Him to help us be confident. Instead of thinking about the greatness of the day, He desires us to give Him glory for creating it.

Communion with the Lord will never happen if we do not actually open up our lives to Him. Yes, He knows every bit of your life, but something powerful happens when we intentionally tell Him about ourselves; when we intentionally come to Him with our concerns… and joys.

But this is a hard habit to form. Trust me.

Luckily, I have found an incredibly helpful tool: talking to God *out loud*. It insures that my thoughts are not just thoughts, but words directed to my Savior. When I pray out loud, there is an element of my spiritual life that seems very tangible and real; I actually sense that Jesus himself is with me.

And as I speak out my praises, thoughts, and concerns, they are all made real to me as well. I take ownership of my feeling of shame and the fact that I need help in it.

There is something truly mystical in voicing prayers to God. However confusing it may be, scripture says that as we pray to the

Father, the Spirit is at work praying through us. So as we address God, He is addressing Himself as well.

When this is done out loud, Satan flees and the Spirit of the Lord is heard through us. I don't know about you, but this is amazing stuff. Not only this, but I believe that this is what God desires for our relationship with Him to be like.

In fact, we see this throughout scripture.

Moses speaks aloud to God in the burning bush; each of the Old Testament prophets address Yahweh out loud; David consistently sings, shouts, and laments to the Lord; the angels in scripture are always seen chanting God's praises; Jesus and the disciples heal and break strongholds through outward prayers; and Paul tells us to "call" on the name of the Lord to be saved.

Although I would love to expound on this more, I can only give you testimony to how life-changing this has been in my own journey. Praying aloud, although awkward at first, allows our actions to match our inner belief that Jesus is real; that He is who we say He is.

Yes, think about it. If we keep our words to Jesus locked up in our mind, this never allows us to experience Him outside of ourselves. But when we speak, wherever we are, we are acknowledging His realness, His providence, and His glory.

Maybe your dryness is a result of your silence to the Lord. Although you think many thoughts, how many of them do you actually present to God? Practice out loud prayers. Practice disclosing who you are to your Savior.

He is calling for us to commune with Him; He actually *wants* to speak with us. But first, we must ask ourselves is if we are ready and willing to stop feeling foundationless emotion and to start listening and speaking to our Lord.

When God's presence is experienced, shame ends. What do you need to do today in order to experience His presence?

QUESTIONS FOR REFLECTION

1. Before reading this chapter, how would you have described your closeness to God? Would it be in terms of your last great experience?

2. Look back on a time in your life where you had a "period of apparent spiritual stagnation, a time in which you didn't feel as if you were going anywhere, a time of dryness and darkness?" (This could very well be now). Reflecting back, can you see where God was at work?
   If not, pray that He would reveal Himself to you.

3. Have you had a recurring thought that could be the Holy Spirit in you? If so, what has it been?

4. Read John 15:1-11. Use this passage to practice the four steps of *lectio divina*. Take time and journal your experience through this.

5. Although it is a hard habit to form, start now and practice the discipline of praying aloud.

CHAPTER 14

ENDURING WITH HIS FULLNESS

*"If you scorn the fellowship of the brethren,
you reject the call of Jesus Christ, and thus
your solitude can only be hurtful to you...."*
-Unknown

*"Christian brotherhood is not an ideal
which we must realize; it is rather a
reality created by God in Christ in
which we may participate...."*
-Dietrich Bonhoeffer

The end is coming.

Although I would love to say something witty and apocalyptic right about now, we both know what I am speaking of. You have finally made it to the last chapter and, soon enough, you will put this book down for good and continue on with your life.

First, kudos to you.

Second, know that you are not yet finished. The truths that are included in this chapter are vital to our battle out of shame. So vital, in fact, that shame will constantly seem to return to our hearts if we do not spend a lifetime applying them. And because I do enjoy ending things on a big note, I have decided to wait until now to speak of these truths.

So here they are.

Shame, the deepest form of it, can *only* be healed through a consistently vulnerable encounter and walk with the fullness of Jesus. And yes, I worded this in a way that will require you to most likely read it again and again.

Our shame will not vanish without the fullness of Jesus permeating our whole self. The funny thing is that we can seek communion with the Lord, receive a self-given "A" for putting Chapter 13 into practice, and yet completely miss this fullness of Jesus that I am speaking of now.

In the letter to the Church of Ephesus, Paul defines this fullness in a very specific way:

> And God placed all things under His [Jesus'] feet and appointed Him to be head over everything for the church, which is His body, the fullness of Him who fills everything in every way.
>
> -Ephesians 1:22-23

The reign of Jesus is for His people, the very people who Paul says make up His fullness. In other words, when the people of the Lord are present, Jesus is *fully* present as well.

This is a concept that we have touched on in earlier chapters, but now it is time to hash it out. For our shame and false beliefs will never leave us without a consistently vulnerable encounter and walk with other believers.

The fact is that you and I and the people around us cannot do this alone. It is through relationships with other believers that the separating power of shame is broken; not only in your heart, but also in theirs.

Where shame pushes us out in isolation, a community pulls us in toward loving grace. Where shame constructs walls, barriers, and fortresses around the heart, a community exercises the beauty and joy of freedom. Where shame belittles our identity and limits our overall potential, a community highlights our true name and calling. And where shame focuses highly on the self, a community focuses on God's Kingdom advancement.

For Jesus is *fully* present when His people are together.

And change can only take place inside of that fullness. In fact, Robert Mulholland defines spiritual formation as being "for the sake of others." So as we experience growth out of shame, we will automatically help others experience it as well.

This is the beautiful work that Satan wants to destroy. He does whatever he can to trick us into thinking that it is "me" against the world; that "my" walk with God is simply mine. But if we are to silence Satan's accusation, then we must be a part of and play a role in God's fullness.

Dying to Our Self

In the Gospels, we see Jesus directing His attention toward His disciples and proclaiming this very familiar statement:

> If anyone would come after me, he must deny himself
> and take up his cross and follow me.
>
> -Matthew 16:24

Many of us may have heard this verse in the context of the "cost of discipleship," but hardly ever as powerful means toward battling shame. But if we are to discover a life with Jesus, one that is wrapped up in His presence and without Satan's accusations, then we must learn to deny ourselves.

And in this context, Jesus is harping on our controlling tendency toward *individuality*. This is the voice inside of us that constantly tells us that we do not need anyone but ourselves; that our life just needs *us* in order for things to get straight.

But if we are to truly follow Jesus, we must deny ourselves and take up *our* cross daily.

This means denying our view of who we are on our own, while stepping into a life that is hidden in Christ; a life that is also full of other people who are hidden in Christ. It means accepting that we do not have it all figured out and denying the part of us that longs to figure it all out. This is because all around us are people that God has given to us as help.

But this is so anti-cultural. In fact, the ruler of this fallen world specializes in keeping our minds on ourselves and keeping our shame deep inside.

We see this type of individuality every day; people who are completely closed off from the world around them. They are the ones that shrink back when questions begin pinpointing their true feelings, shift into a frenzy of obnoxious jokes when the conversation becomes too heavy, or even avoid all environments that feel out of their comfort and control.

These people are living in isolation; people much like you and me. Although a loving church may surround us, our "individual" tendency keeps us from truly denying our own agenda in order to be with these people. And in doing this, our actions communicate a deep belief that we do not need them.

In our shame, our minds are focused only on ourselves. Let me say that again: in our shame, our minds are focused *only on ourselves*. We have become self-centered and prideful. But in following a God that demands oneness and sacrificial love, a focus like this seems pretty strange.

Yet we still wonder why *we* feel so alone; why no one around us seems to care; and why our church feels so unloving.

But what if the answers to these questions lie in our refusal to truly deny all aspects of ourselves? What if these feelings sprout from a perspective that is very *me* centered? And what if the very reason for our continual shame is because we have yet to let it surface to those closest to us?

Living alone, many times, is our choosing. But so is the daily decision of denying ourselves and living together.

True Honesty

Although I am still very young, I have been blessed with the opportunity to lead some amazing small groups. They have been experiences that have not only allowed me to pour into others, but have also exponentially grown my own walk with Christ.

The most successful group that I have been a part of was the one that I began leading during my sophomore year in college. This group consisted of eight freshman guys, all of whom I am still close to today.

But in no way do I contribute this success to myself. It belongs fully to the Spirit's love of using people's honesty and vulnerability. In fact, those men were the reason that growth continued; for they regularly committed to be genuine with one another.

And it all began the first night of meeting with each other. Even though my heart was pounding and my pits were sweating, I decided that night to open up and let them into all aspects of who I was. I denied any fears regarding my years of shame and laid it all on the table: "This is who Greg is and where he came from."

And what happened after that first time together was of most significance to me; it was a defining moment in my own battle of shame. After everyone left, one of the guys stayed back and asked if he could talk with me.

Unaware of what was going to be said, I quickly agreed. As we began talking, the Lord began working. This freshman opened up and spoke of his deep shame, a shame that was very close to my own. He told me how powerful it was to hear someone else's journey through it and how amazed he was at my own vulnerability.

That night, he became vulnerable.

And even though he looks back at that conversation as a time where I helped him, the truth is that it was a moment of complete victory for me—one that *he* blessed me with. It was in that moment that I knew that God worked through my shame. If I had not been vulnerable, I would have never been able to recognize the true extent of victory in my own life. It was a beautiful picture of Jesus' treasure shining through my outer clay.

That night I learned that sharing my shameful past reminds me that it is not me. It reminds my own heart that I have been delivered and made whole in Christ Jesus. This truth has carried me through many other vulnerable moments where my heart has pounded and my pits have sweated.

After setting this foundation of honesty, this group of guys began being a *real* group. My vulnerability led toward them showing vulnerability, and together, we shared our shame and recognized our victory.

You see, honesty and vulnerability always breed transformation. There is divine power in sharing our struggles, our sins, and our mishaps. And this power is beyond us; beyond anything we could ever discover on our own. The Apostle Paul refers to this as boasting about our weaknesses:

> Therefore I will boast all the more gladly about my weaknesses, so that Christ's power may rest on me. That is why, for Christ's sake, I delight in weaknesses, in insults, in hardships, in persecutions, in difficulties. For when I am weak, then I am strong.
> -2 Corinthians 12:9-10

In some weird and beautiful way, the Lord delights in our display of weakness. Paul even writes that it is "for Christ's sake" that we delight in our shortcomings.

Although this is true, there is a fine line with this. You see, boasting in our weaknesses reveals Christ's power, not our own. And the end result of sharing our shame is never to make ourselves *appear* holier, but instead, to give glory to Jesus Christ.

When we are genuinely weak, He will be seen. And when we are genuinely weak, our hearts will be uncovered—not revealing how shameful or worthless we are, but how victorious and strong we have become in Jesus Christ. This not only blesses our hearers, but also enlightens our eyes to see God's grace in us.

Bearing Burdens

In high school, I was full of burdens; years of hidden sexual sins that had me tied up like a ball of rubber bands. And on top of all of this was a huge entanglement of the guilt and shame of not being a good son.

During my senior year, my mother passed away from breast cancer. It was soon after that I realized my shoulders were heavy with every missed opportunity that was now behind me. I constantly regretted how little time I spent with her and how very little love I seemed to give to her.

Although every bit of this made me want to retreat deeper and deeper into myself, the Lord blessed me with someone who continually fought alongside me.

He was the intern for my youth group, but to me, he was my first true mentor. This guy dug deep into my shame and carried every bit of it with me. He taught me to live with and proclaim my weaknesses instead of seeking to cover them up with false strength. Through it all, he walked with me.

Without a doubt, his wise words blessed my life.

But if you asked him today about those two years, he would say that his words to me were really God's words to him; that even though God gave him to me as means of growth, God also gave me to him for growth.

You see, my mentor had shame of his own. Although he never would have labeled it as shame, there were dozens of lies in him that told him he was forever unworthy. But every time he served me through carrying my burdens, the Holy Spirit would somehow gracefully carry his own.

And there is a valuable lesson in this.

Although it may sound odd, one of the best ways to end the shame in our own life is to battle it alongside others. When we serve one another in this way, Jesus' fullness is truly experienced and seen. For Paul writes that Jesus' attitude, being God, was of a servant; that He came to "serve, not to be served" (Mark 10:45).

So in serving me, my mentor was acting *like* Jesus.

This does not mean that we neglect our own shame, but instead, we work through it as we serve and work through the shame in others. It takes into account that we are weak, yet divinely powerful. When my mentor truly battled with my shame, he experienced God's victory in his own heart.

To the Galatians, Paul writes this:

> Since we live by the Spirit, let us keep in step with the Spirit… Brothers, if someone is caught in a sin, you who are spiritual should restore him gently. But watch yourself, or you also may be tempted. Carry each other's burdens, and in this way you will fulfill the law of Christ.
>
> -Galatians 5:25; 6:1-2

Because *we* live by the Spirit, *we*—you and I together—should keep in step with Him. Paul's commands are for these people to not only deny themselves, but to actually dive into each other's struggles.

And it is the same for us today. We should carry one another's burdens while restoring each other gently.

Because this is not about neglecting our shame, but embracing the victory in it, Paul writes for us to constantly watch ourselves; to watch our intentions and motives. When bearing with others, we should never forget that we, ourselves, have burdens to be carried.

The beauty in this is that many times, like my mentor, God will use our words given for others to dramatically shape us. For in a life of service, the Spirit will transform us.

But all of this requires intentionality.

You will never bear other people's hardships, burdens, and shame on accident. And you will never "just happen" to get someone to be vulnerable with you. It demands for you to intentionally carry your cross and live a life of honesty yourself.

This is where we come full circle. Hopefully, by now, you have taken many of the truths in this book to thought. But to ultimately apply them to your life is to share them with others. Bear with those closest to you by fighting their shame with your own, and together, experience Jesus' fullness.

Final Thoughts

Although I leave with this last charge, my prayer is that you continually take the truths and practical steps in this book and apply them to your life. In no way do I take credit for the work that God has done and will do through this book.

Much like my mentor's words to me, these chapters have been a major source of growth in my own life. The words that I have written have countlessly smacked me in my own face and will continue to do so.

Therefore, I pray that it blesses you as it has blessed me.

But now I would like to finish right where we began.

Let us always remember that we are jars of clay, not housing the shame and taint of sin and brokenness, but an all-powerful treasure that was graciously given to us. In our battle with shame, this is the truth that we hold tightly to:

> For God, who said, "Let light shine out of darkness," made His light shine in our hearts to give us the light of the knowledge of the glory of God in the face of Christ. But we have this treasure in jars of clay to show that this all-surpassing power is from God and not from us. We are hard pressed on every side, but not

crushed, perplexed, but not in despair; persecuted, but not abandoned; struck down, but not destroyed. We always carry in our body the death of Jesus, so that the life of Jesus may also be revealed in our body...life is at work in you.

                                    -2 Corinthians 4:5-10; 12

QUESTIONS FOR REFLECTION

1. Who are the people that God has used to speak into your own life? Who are the people that God has used you to speak to?

2. Has your shame isolated you from those around you? How can you practice *dying to self?*

3. Have you experienced victory from being vulnerable about your sin and shame? If so write it out. If not, I challenge you to experience it soon.

4. Who is someone in your life that you feel called to fight alongside of? Have you discovered their burdens? If so, how can you "bear their burdens" today?

INDEX AND SOURCES

Preface: What You Need to Know

"But we have": 2 Corinthians 4:7 (NIV)

"For God, who": 2 Corinthians 4:6-10; 12 (NIV)

Chapter 1: Do You Feel It?

"Shame is a": Jung, C.G. Excerpt from *The Red Book*.

"Smedes": Smedes, L. B. (1993). *Shame and Grace: Healing the Shame We Don't Deserve*. New York, NY: Random House Publishing.

"And a leper": Mark 1:40-42 (NASB)

Chapter 2: Healthy Shame

"Woe is me": Isaiah 6:5 (NASB)

"Holy, Holy, Holy": Isaiah 6:3 (NASB)

"Then one of the": Isaiah 6:6-7 (NIV)

"Smedes": Smedes, L. B. (1993). *Shame and Grace: Healing the Shame We Don't Deserve*. New York, NY: Random House Publishing.

"Then I heard": Isaiah 6:8 (NASB)

Chapter 3: Unhealthy Shame

"You can find": Rushdie, S. (1983). *Shame: A Novel*. New York, NY: St. Martin's Press.

"Mine has been": Dazai, O. (1958). *No Longer Human*. New York, NY: New Directions Publishing Corporation.

"You killed the": Excerpt from Walt Disney Pictures, *The Lion King*.

"Run away and": Excerpt from Walt Disney Pictures, *The Lion King.*

"Body of Christ": See 1 Corinthians 12:12-31, Colossians 1:18, or Romans 12:4-5.

"Fullness of God": Ephesians 1:22-23 (NIV)

"I pray that": Ephesians 1:18-19 (NIV)

"Hakuna Matata": Excerpt from Walt Disney Pictures, *The Lion King.*

Chapter 4: The "Shamer" and His Tactics

"By mixing a": C.S. Lewis

"The devil is": Thomas Adams

"Morning star": Isaiah 14:12-15

"Steal, kill, and destroy": John 10:10

"Filthy, two legged": Lewis, C. S. (1942). *The Screwtape Letters.* New York, NY: HarperCollins Publishers.

"Jamieson, Fausset, and Brown": Jamieson, R., Fausset, A. R., & Brown, D. (1997). *Commentary Critical and Explanatory on the Whole Bible.* (Heb 3:13). Oak Harbor, WA: Logos Research Systems, Inc.

Chapter 5: The Way We Once Were

"In the image": Genesis 1:27; 2:25 (NIV)

"Then God said": Genesis 1:26-28; 31(NASB)

"For by Him": Colossans 1:16-17 (NIV)

Chapter 6: When Perfection Became Ashamed

"Then the eyes": Genesis 3:7 (NASB)

"In the knowledge": Bonhoeffer, D. (1955). *Ethics.* New York, NY: Touchstone.

"Now the Serpent": Genesis 3:1 (NRSV)

"Did God really": Genesis 3:1-5 (NRSV)

"Then the eyes": Genesis 3:7 (NASB)

"Dietrich Bonhoeffer": Bonhoeffer, D. (1955).

"Man covers himself": Bonhoeffer, D. (1955).

"The earth is defiled": Isaiah 24:5-6 (NIV)

Chapter 7: The Shame Bearer

"For our sake": 2 Corinthians 5:21 (NRSV)

"In Him was": John 1:4-5; 9-10 (ESV)

"World did not recognize Him": See John 1:10 (NIV)

"Yet to all": John 1:12-13 (NIV)

"Darkness again..": See John 12:35 (NIV)

"Put your trust": John 12:36 (NIV)

"My soul is": Mark 14:34 (NIV)

"Father, if You": Luke 22:42 (ESV)

"And being in": Luke 22:44 (ESV)

Chapter 8: We Now Stand Unashamed

"Outside of Christ": Watchman Nee, an excerpt from his biography.

"I pray also": John 17:20-23 (NIV)

"We were therefore": Romans 6:4-5, 7 (NIV)

"Disarmed the power": See Colossians 2:15

"Sin is no longer our master": See Galatians 4 & 5

"Who shall separate": Romans 8:35-39 (NIV)

"That can never": 1 Peter 1:4 (NIV)

"Shielded": 1 Peter 1:5 (NIV)

"See, my Servant": Isaiah 52:13-14; 53:7-11 (NIV)

"Do not be afraid": Isaiah 54:4-5 (NIV)

"Participate in that": 2 Peter 1:4 (NIV)

"No weapon forged": Isaiah 54:17 (NIV)

"Servants of righteousness": See Romans 6:18

"Our benefits in Christ": See Romans 6:21-22

Chapter 9: The Blameless Life

"Great was thy": Bennett, A. (2007). *The Valley of Vision: A Collection of Puritan Prayers & Devotions.* (p. 99). Carlisle, PA: The Banner of Truth Trust.

"Satan approaches the": See Job 1

"Committed to us": See 2 Corinthians 5

"For this reason": 2 Peter 1:5-8 (NIV)

Chapter 10: Searching Deep

"Search me, God": Psalm 139:23-24 (NIV)

"Shoulding on": Ellis, A., & Abrams, M. (2009). *Personality Theories: Critical Perspectives.* Thousand Oaks, CA: SAGE Publications, Inc.

"Life to the fullest": see John 10:10

"Am I now": Galatians 1:10 (NIV)

Chapter 11: Gracing Ourselves

"I have learned": Excerpt from JoyBell, C. C. (2012). *The Sun is Snowing: Poems, Parables and Pictures.* USA: Author House.

"I was reading an article": findings from Ahmed, E., & Braithwaite, V. (2006). Forgiveness, Reconciliation, and Shame: Three Key Variables in Reducing School Bullying. *Journal of Social Issues, 62* (2), 347-370.

"See to it": Hebrews 12:15 (NRSV)

"The God of": Romans 16:20 (NIV)

"What then?": Romans 6:15 (NIV)

"Now that you": Romans 6:22 (NIV)

"It is in": U.S Catholic (2008). Apology Accepted. *PracticingCatholic*, *37-8.*

Chapter 12: Pursuing Positive Pleasures

"God whispers to": Excerpt from Lewis, C.S. (1999). *The Problem With Pain: A Grief Observed.* Nashville, TN: Broadman & Holman Publishers.

"Very truly I": John 13:38 (NIV)

"John writes that:": See John 21

"The deepest likings": Excerpt from Lewis, C.S. (1942). *The Screwtape Letters.* New York, NY: HarperCollins Publishers.

"Raw material": Excerpt from Lewis, C.S. (1942). *The Screwtape Letters.*

"It was rather": Henry, M. (1994). *Matthew Henry's Commentary on the Whole Bible: Complete and Unabridged in One Volume* (p. 2056). Peabody: Hendrickson.

"When they had finished": John 21:15-17 (NRSV)

"How can you": Lewis, C.S. (1942). *The Screwtape Letters.*

"The man who": Lewis, C.S. (1942). *The Screwtape Letters.*

"The great thing": Lewis, C.S. (1942). *The Screwtape Letters.*

Chapter 13: The Call for Communion

"I live in": Excerpt from Ernest Holmes's *The Science of the Mind*

"What we don't": Mulholland, R. (1993). *Invitation to a Journey: A Road Map For Spiritual Formation.* Downers Grove, IL: InterVarsity Press.

"When I seek": Willard, D. (2012). *Hearing God: Developing a Conversational Relationship With God.* Downers Grove, IL: InterVarsity Press.

"We have the": 1 Corinthians 2:16

"We must not": Willard, D. (2012). *Hearing God: Developing a Conversational Relationship With God.* Downers Grove, IL: InterVarsity Press.

Chapter 14: Enduring With His Fullness

"If you scorn": Excerpt from Bonheoffer, D. (1954). *Life Together: A Discussion of Christian Fellowship.* New York, NY: Harper & Row Publishers, Inc.

"Christian brotherhood is": Bonheoffer, D. (1954). *Life Together.: A Discussion of Christian Fellowship.* New York, NY: Harper & Row Publishers, Inc.

"And God placed": Ephesians 1:22-23 (NIV)

"If anyone would": Matthew 16:24 (ESV)

"...Therefore, I will": 2 Corinthians 12:9-10 (NIV)

"Serve, not to": Mark 10:45

"Since we live": Galatians 5:25; 6:1-2 (NIV)

"For God, who": 2 Corinthians 4:5-10; 12 (NIV)

Sources of Reference:

Anderson, N. T. (2000). *The Bondage Breaker.* Eugene, OR: Harvest House Publishing

Ashby, J. S., Rice, K. G., & Martin, J. L. (2006). Perfectionism, Shame, and Depressive Symptoms. *Journal of Counseling & Development, 84(2).*

Bennett, A. (2007). *The Valley of Vision: A Collection of Puritan Prayers & Devotions.* Carlisle, PA: The Banner of Truth Trust.

Bonhoeffer, D. (1955). *Ethics.* New York, NY: Touchstone.

Easton, M. G. (1996). *Easton's Bible Dictionary.* Oak Harbor, WA: Logos Research Systems, Inc.

Freeman, J. M., & Chadwick, H. J. (1998). *Manners & Customs of the Bible.* North Brunswick, NJ: Bridge-Logos Publishers.

Fuller, L. K. (2008). Perfectionism and Shame: Exploring the Connections. *Journal of Pastoral Theology, 18*(1), 44-60.

Guigo, I. (1981). *The Ladder of Monks and Twelve Meditations.* Kalamazoo: Cistercian Publications.

Jamieson, R., Fausset, A. R., & Brown, D. (1997). *Commentary Critical and Explanatory on the Whole Bible.* Oak Harbor, WA: Logos Research Systems, Inc.

Leon Wurmser, "Shame, The Veiled Companion of Narcissism," in The Many Faces of Shame, ed. Nathanson, 67-68

Lewis, C. S. (1942). *The Screwtape Letters.* New York, NY: HarperCollins Publishers.

Lewis, H. B. 1971. *Shame and Guilt in Neurosis.* International University Press. New York.

Lewis, M. (1992). *Shame: The Exposed Self.* New York, NY: The Free Press.

McConnell, J. M., & Dixon, D. (2012). Perceived Forgiveness from God and Self-forgiveness. *Journal of Psychology and Christianity 2012.*

Nathanson, D., ed. (1987) *The Many Faces of Shame.* New York, NY: The Guild ford Press.

Ortberg, J. (2002). *The Life You've Always Wanted: Spiritual Disciplines for Ordinary People.* Grand Rapids, MI: Zondervan.

Pembroke, N. (2012). Pastoral Care for Shame-based Perfectionism. *Pastoral Psychology, 61*(2), 245-258. doi:10.1007/s11089-011-0414-z

Smedes, L. B. (1993). *Shame and Grace: Healing the Shame We Don't Deserve.* New York, NY: Random House Publishing.

Strassner, K. (2009). *Opening up Genesis*. Opening Up Commentary. Leominster: Day One Publications.

Stiebert, J. (2002). *The Construction of Shame in the Hebrew Bible: The Prophetic Contribution*. Shattfield Academic Press.

Swanson, J. (1997). *Dictionary of Biblical Languages with Semantic Domains: Hebrew (Old Testament)* (electronic ed.). Oak Harbor: Logos Research Systems, Inc.

Tangney, J., & Dearing, R. (2002). *Shame and Guilt*. New York, NY: The Guilford Press.

Utley, R. J. (2001). *Vol. Vol. 1A: How it All Began: Genesis 1–11*. Study Guide Commentary Series. Marshall, Texas: Bible Lessons International.

Velleman, J. D. (2001), The Genesis of Shame. Philosophy & Public Affairs, 30: 27–52. doi: 10.1111/j.1088-4963.2001.00027.x

Wood, D. R. W., & Marshall, I. H. (1996). *New Bible Dictionary* (3rd ed.). Leicester, England; Downers Grove, IL: InterVarsity Press.